DOUGGIE'S
SUPER
SCIENCE
ADVENTURES

DOUGGIE'S SUPER SCIENCE ADVENTURES

Stories for Teaching the Next Generation Science Standards for Third Graders

MICHAEL BRUMAGE

ARPress
ILLUMINATING IDEAS.
EMPOWERING VOICES

ARPress
45 Dan Road Suite 5
Canton MA 02021

Hotline: 1(800) 220-7660
Fax: 1(855) 752-6001

Ordering Information:
Quantity sales. Special discounts are available on quantity purchases by corporations, associations, and others. For details, contact the publisher at the address above.

Printed in the United States of America.

| ISBN-13: | Softcover | 979-8-89356-461-7 |
| | eBook | 979-8-89356-460-0 |

Library of Congress Control Number: 2024904604

Table Of Contents

ACKNOWLEDGMENTS

This book is a collection of shorts stories inspired by my life as a teacher and a father of three children. As a science teacher by profession, I have tried to encourage my children to learn to find answers to their own questions by using the resources available to them. Their curiosity and amazing questions have inspired the character of Douggie. I have learned so much from them. I want to thank my amazing wife Aimee for her long hours spent editing and proofreading the stories. Her positive feedback encouraged me to continue writing them. I also want to thank my kids, Ellie, Livya and Oliver, for their patience and inspiration. They allow me to work and write without too many interruptions, and they willingly read the stories and provided much needed feedback. To Ellie, my oldest, I want to thank her for all of her beautiful illustrations.

To my friends who have encouraged me to get these books published, I thank you for believing in me and in this project. I also want to thank my teachers through the years who have inspired me to give back to education. They have given so much to me and have encouraged me to be a lifelong learner. I want all teachers to know they are appreciated and are touching lives every day.

INTRODUCTION

When the next generation science standards came out, I realized that there were a high number of teachers who were not excited about the changes. For many elementary teachers it is a scary thought to have to teach these new, complex science standards. As a teacher of science for 16 years, I realized that I could offer them something they needed and didn't have. I decided to provide these stories to be used to introduce and explain each new science standard. The lessons that Douggie learns can help each person understand the science of each standard as they read the stories and become absorbed in the adventures and investigations along with Douggie. The activities Douggie and his parents engage in can encourage both teachers and students to dive deeper into these complex standards and the scientific knowledge associated with them. I have often found that my students get more out of one of my "stories with a point" than taking notes from a lecture. Stories touch us personally by drawing from our own memories. This fact can help us recall the scientific point and even apply it in different real-life situations. The questions at the end are designed as jumping-off points and can be used to encourage whole class discussions about the scientific applications of these standards.

My hope is that these stories will bring out the little Douggie in all of us by encouraging us to keep asking questions and seeking answers to these questions, without being afraid to try new things. There is so much information at our fingertips and no reason to give up our quest for knowledge. Being a lifelong learner doesn't stop. The world is amazing; all we have to do is look.

I often reflect back on the stories I tell my class and use them reinforce a concept. These stories can and should be used in a similar fashion by teachers, parents and students. Enjoy.

Chapter 1

SHORTS OR PANTS?

*ESS2-1: Represent data in tables and graphical
displays to describe typical weather conditions
expected during a particular season.*

Little Douggie is fascinated with the world around him. He has always been very curious and full of questions. Finding the answers to his questions is not always easy, so he tends to seek help from his parents. His mother and father love their little Douggie, but they admit that all his questions can take their toll, so they started helping him find the answers to his questions instead of answering them directly. Douggie's parents take him to local museums, science centers, and the library. They even search the internet to help him explore and find the answers to his questions. Still, more often than not, the answers only lead to more questions.

Douggie and his parents were looking forward to spring break and their vacation in Southern California. They used the weekend before spring break to pack and prepare the house for their week away.

Douggie wondered how he should pack for the trip. "Mom, do I need to pack pants and a jacket?" he asked, hoping his mother would answer, "No."

Instead, she countered, "We need to check to see what kind of weather they are expecting to have during our stay in Southern California."

"Can we do that now? I really need to get my packing finished," Douggie stated with a serious look on his face. His mother smiled, wondering to herself where he got all his motivation and energy.

"Let's look online and see if we can get some information on the forecast for that area," his mother said, as she began booting up the computer. "I really ought to have done this earlier," his mother added with a small look of regret on her face.

"No worries, Mom. This should be a snap," Douggie said with a smile and his usual enthusiasm. "I have a feeling that the temperature will be perfect, and I am hoping no storms will be coming in," Douggie continued.

The weather forecast for Catalina Island was in the 80's during the days, with clear skies. The lows were expected to be in the high 50's or low 60's with early morning fog, clearing by mid-morning. No rain was predicted during their stay. "I don't think the weather could be more perfect for our vacation," his mother stated.

"This could be a good time to visit almost any place, don't you think, Mom?" Douggie asked as they moved away from the computer. That made Douggie start thinking about what the temperature would be during the other three seasons. He knew what the weather was where he lived, but he was curious about the weather in other places around California. His mother always said California had virtually every type of climate. He wanted to be able to somehow gather this information together and compare the each of the locations during the all four seasons.

He decided to get his journal and write down a simple table with the four seasons on it. He listed the four seasons along the bottom of the graph, and the temperature ranges ran up the graph's left side. He included three locations in California: His hometown, Catalina Island, and Palm Springs, where his grandparents lived. He picked out a specific sticker for each location. Palm Springs got a palm tree sticker. For his hometown, Douggie decided to use a sticker of a house, and for Catalina he chose island-shaped stickers.

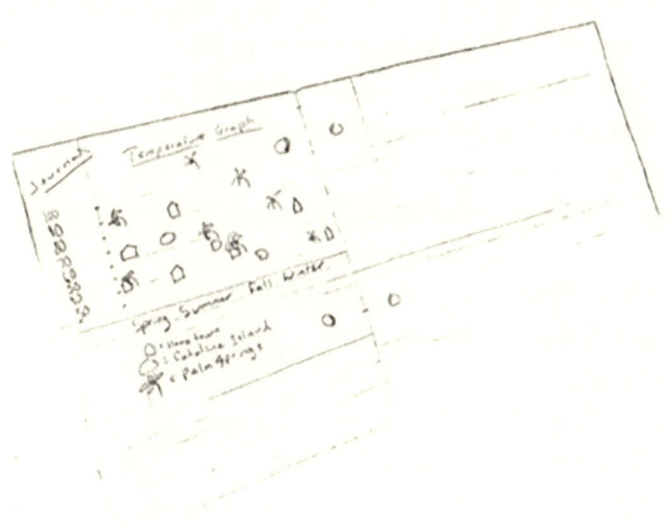

The next thing for him to do was to enlist a parent to help him look online for the information he needed.

"I already got help from Mom this morning, so I think I will see what Dad is doing," Douggie said to himself. He found his father trying to reset the timer on the sprinkler system in the garage. "Dad, when you have a few minutes, can you help me find a little information online?" Douggie asked as politely as he could. He knew if he asked nicely, even when his father was busy, he would be likely to get the help he needed. "Sure, no problem," his father responded after a brief pause. "I need to take a break from dealing with this silly thing anyway." "What is it you need help finding online?" his father asked.

"I would like to know what the weather is during different times of the year in our town, on Catalina Island and in Palm Springs, where Gammy lives," Douggie responded with a sheepish look on his face.

His father looked at him and smiled and said, "Douggie, this isn't exactly the strangest thing you have asked me to help you with, but it's close." They both walked over to the computer monitor and sat down. His dad began typing in the information.

"I guess we will start with our hometown," his father stated. Douggie nodded in agreement. Douggie had his pencil and journal ready. "The average high during the winter time is 65° F and the average low is 40°," his father began. "The average rainfall is approximately four inches in the winter."

Douggie looked up and said, "That sounds right, don't you think, Dad?"

"I think so. Let's keep going," said his father. "In the springtime, the average highs are in the high 70's to low 80's, and the average lows are in the 60's."

"Keep reading, Dad. This is great," Douggie urged his father, as his pencil busily scribbled in his journal.

Douggie's father continued: "In the summertime, the average highs are in the 90's and the lows are in the mid 60's. There isn't very much rainfall in the summertime. The average rainfall is around half an inch."

"Our summers are very dry," Douggie added.

"No doubt," his father agreed. "That's why I need those sprinklers working correctly. That reminds me, I still have to finish in the garage, so let's get this done," his father said, trying not to sound too impatient. "The fall temperatures range from the highs in the mid 70's to the lows in the high 50's and low 60's. The rainfall averages around two inches during this time," his father said as he finished reading that page of information.

"What town should we do next?" his father asked, trying to hurry things along.

"I want to look at Catalina Island next," Douggie responded. "Okay, let's see what we can find," his father stated as he typed away on the keyboard. Douggie's father found a website that explained Catalina Island's temperature ranges. As Douggie's father read from the website, Douggie was busy listening and taking notes in his journal.

"In the summertime the average high is in the mid 70's and the lows are in the low 60's. Those temperatures continue into November, where the lows start dipping into the high 50's."

"Dad, the temperature doesn't & much at all during the summer. While other places are getting hot and unbearable, Catalina is perfect." "Agreed, but I bet living there can be expensive. I bet they pay top dollar to live in such a beautiful place," his father added then continued reading from the web site. "During the wintertime, the average temperature ranges from the highs in the mid 60's to the lows in the 50's. The island gets almost all of its rainfall during winter, with an average of 15 inches each year, according to the website."

"The winter time probably wouldn't be the best time to visit the island," Douggie said, knowing his father was thinking the same thing. "That's what I was thinking," his father said. "This website indicates that springtime on Catalina Island has the least amount of precipitation, and temperatures range from the mid 70's to low 60's.

"That's when we get to go. It should be perfect!" Douggie stated with excitement.

Douggie's father was ready to be done, but he knew he had one more city to look up for Douggie. "So, Palm Springs, is it?" his father asked, checking to make sure Douggie was still interested in that city.

"Oh, yes," Douggie responded. "I'll bet it is quite different from the ones we have just looked at."

Douggie's father had already begun typing at the keyboard, hoping to finish quickly and get back to his sprinklers. "It says here Palm Springs has almost no rainfall at all. Fewer than 4 inches a year, and recently it's been closer to 2 inches per year," read his dad.

"But everything is lush and green there. It's hard to believe they only get around 2 inches of rain," Douggie stated with a perplexed look on his face. His father explained how people in Palm Springs need to rely on their sprinklers to keep things green, and not the rain.

Douggie's dad continued to read off the weather information for Douggie. Together they learned the average temperatures during the winter in Palm Springs range from the low 40's to the low 70's. Temperatures in the fall and spring range between highs in the 80's and 90's, and lows in the mid 50's to mid 60's. In the summer, temperatures reach the 100's, with highs around 105° and lows in the high 70's.

"That is too hot for me," Douggie stated.

"Everyone who lives there has an air conditioner," his father said with a smile and a little chuckle.

"I guess so. Gammy said a neighbor of hers dropped an egg on the sidewalk, and by the time she got back to clean it up, it had already cooked, just as it would in a pan on the stove," Douggie said, wondering what his father would say in response.

"That's how I cook my eggs when I'm in Palm Springs," his dad responded with a twinkle in his eye and little smile.

"I have to get back to my sprinklers. Have you got what you needed son?"

"Yes. Thank you for your help Dad, good luck with the sprinklers." Douggie decided to make a large chart using the graph from his journal to make it easier to understand. Luckily he had plenty of stickers to create the large chart. He even had the same stickers in both blue and red.

"I think I will use the red for the highs and the blue for the lows," Douggie stated to himself. This would allow Douggie to use three different shapes of stickers representing the three locations, the houses, the islands and the palm trees, with two different colors to use for the highs and lows for each.

Douggie gave each season a reading of a high and a low for each of the three locations. The seasons started with spring and went through to winter. When he was done, he realized he had created a chart he could hang on the wall clearly showing the ranges of temperatures in all three locations. Without hesitating, Douggie gathered four thumb tacks and hung it up on his wall then stepped back.

"I think I will invite Gammy to my house this summer. Palm Springs is too hot for me." Douggie said to himself, as he looked at the extremes of temperatures on his chart.

Remembering his empty suitcase and the packing he had yet to finish, Douggie came to a reasonable conclusion. "It looks like I will need a light jacket and some pants for the evenings on Catalina Island. It gets chilly there at night."

Suddenly another question popped into his mind. "I wonder how cold the ocean is around Catalina Island?" he thought. "I had better wait to ask that one," he decided, as a smile developed on his face.

Questions:

1. What role do you think the ocean plays in the weather, specifically temperatures?
2. What do you think makes Palm Springs hot and dry?
3. Why would winter not be the best time to visit the Island in the story?

Vocabulary:

1. Enthusiasm
2. Sheepish
3. Precipitation

Chapter 2

HOW'S THE WEATHER?

ESS2-2: Obtain and combine information to
describe climates in different regions of the world.

In the first week of each month, Douggie took time to write his pen pals from around the world. He had been writing to his pen pals for as long as he could remember. His mother used to write the notes as he dictated to her, but after he learned to write, he began to write the letters all by himself. The day he had set aside to write his letters had arrived. Recently Douggie had started writing his letters on the computer, printing them out to send or e-mailing the pen pals who had e-mail addresses. His mother said that the idea of sending the letters through regular mail, also known as snail-mail, was really the preferred method even though many people have moved to e-mailing their pen pals.

Douggie's favorite topics to write about were the most recent investigations he had been involved in, as well as the basic stuff, such as the weather and what was new with his friends. He tried to keep his letters to one page because some of his pals had complained in the past about his long letters, saying that they had trouble writing as much in response and that they felt guilty for writing shorter letters.

Each of Douggie's pen pals lived at a military base somewhere around the world. Some were children of members of the military, and others were members of the military themselves. His number of pen pals had grown recently but typically ranged between eight and ten. Douggie had decided to put up a map of the world on his wall showing where his pen pals lived, which helped him keep track of them easily. He had placed a pin in the location of every pen pal, with their names taped to the pins. Some of his pen pals had moved to different locations since he started writing to them.

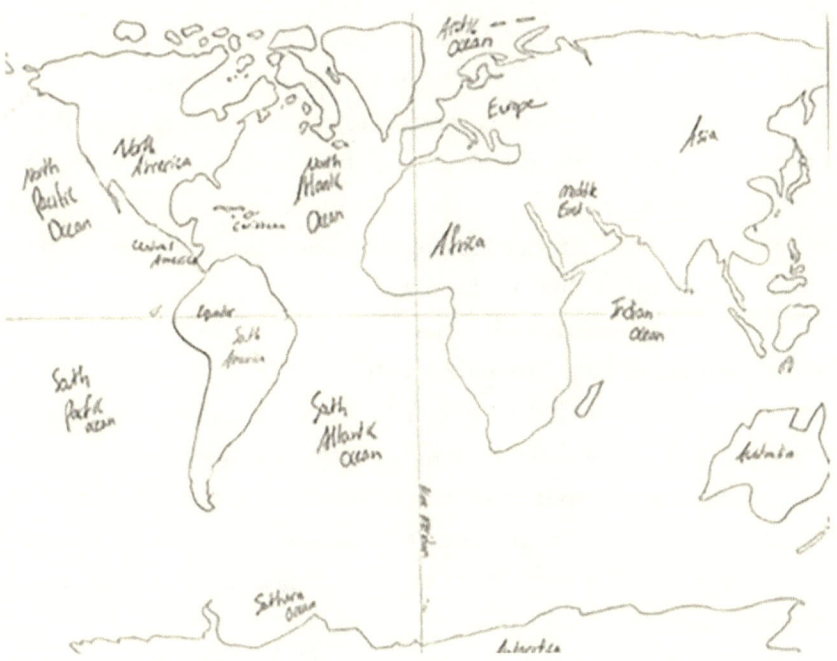

The last letters Douggie received were interesting because they revealed that some of his pen pals had very different weather patterns from the ones he had experienced at his home in California. In the middle of summer, he had a few pen pals who were actually having their winter. Others never really had a summer. All of these differences began to make Douggie wonder how many different types of climates there were in the world.

He remembered his teacher had recently introduced the biomes of the world to his class. He also remembered that they had different types of weather, but he wanted more information about his pen pals' weather specifically. Douggie was hoping he could add information about each of his pen pals' weather to his wall map with help from their letters and the internet. He decided to use a different color for each climate zone. At breakfast Douggie decided to ask his parents for help with his project. "Hey, Mom, Dad, did you know there are different climates in the world?" he asked, as his parents ate their cereal.

His mother looked across the table at him with a smile and responded, "You don't say?"

"Do you know what they are and where they are located?" his father asked, trying to show interest in what his son was saying.

"Not really," Douggie answered, "That's why I need your help. I would like to look up the different climates and show them on my pen pal map. That way I will have more information about where they live and the types of weather they are experiencing. It will help me feel closer to them even though they are far away."

His parents looked at each other. The one to speak first was usually the one drafted to help Douggie on the computer. Douggie's mother smiled and said, "I would love to help you look online. I have a few dishes to finish up, and then I will be with you. Why don't you turn on the computer and sign in so we can start just as soon as I finish up in the kitchen?" She then glanced at his father with a look that hinted that he now owed her a favor. They both smiled, understanding each other perfectly.

Once online, the search was quite easy. Douggie's mother was able to find several websites containing the information they were looking for. Douggie chose the website that made the most sense to him. One that used various colors to show each of the climate zones, just as he wanted to do on his own map.

"How cool! I don't even have to think up the colors myself. The website has them all selected for me," Douggie stated with his usual excitement. "Let me get my journal and I will be ready to go," he said as he ran off to his bedroom.

His mother giggled. "He loves this so much," she said under her breath. When he returned she read the website out loud to Douggie, listing the climate zones as tropical, dry, temperate, cold, and polar. The website also used a classification system broken into three basic groups located in specific latitudes.

"Mom, what does 'latitude' mean?" Douggie asked with a puzzled look on his face.

She asked him to go and get his globe and bring it downstairs to help her explain the concept to him. His mother took the globe and showed him the lines running parallel to the equator, the line in the middle of the planet. "These lines show the latitude in degrees. This globe goes by fifteen-degree increments between each line until it gets to the latitudes 60° and 70°, where it then goes by ten degrees," his mother explained. Douggie was quite satisfied with her explanation, and smiled as they went back to their research.

"The group closest to the equator, or latitude 0°, out to approximately twenty-five degrees north or south of the equator, is called the low-latitude climates. In this grouping, there are three actual climate zones: The moist tropical climates, the wet-dry tropical climates and the dry tropical climates, also known as tropical deserts.

"You mean even though these areas are really close to the equator, they are not all rainforests?" Douggie asked, trying to get this clear in his mind.

"It is amazing, but yes," said Douggie's mother. "There are tropical rain forests, tropical grass lands and tropical deserts. Each one is hot, but they get different amounts of rainfall or precipitation."

"I didn't know that, but it does make sense," said Douggie.

The article mentioned some areas around the world that were in each category. For the tropical rain forests it listed the Amazon basin, the Congo in Africa, and Indonesia, just above Australia. For the wet-dry tropical climates, the article listed India, Western and Southern Africa, parts of South America, and Northern Australia. For the tropical deserts, it listed areas including the middle part of Australia, Southwest United States, North Africa, and South Africa, and Northern Mexico. "I have heard of these places, but now I know generally what their weather is like. This is getting fun!" Douggie added with a smile on his face.

His mother couldn't help agreeing. She was learning a few new things as well. She just didn't want Douggie to know.

Douggie's mother said, "According to the article, the next grouping includes the area between latitudes twenty-five degrees and approximately fifty-five degrees." She explained that this group, called the mid-latitude climates, includes the moist continental climates, the Mediterranean climates and the dry, mid-latitude climates, or grasslands, and the dry mid-latitude desert climates or Steppes.

"Mom," Douggie said. "I think this could get confusing without a globe or a map of the earth."

"I agree. It's nice to have the globe right here in front of us," his mother agreed.

"The article mentions some areas in each category. For the moist continental climates or deciduous forests, the article included the Northeastern part of the U.S., Southern Canada, Korea, Japan and parts of Eastern Europe. For the Mediterranean climates it included areas around the Mediterranean Sea, the West Coast of Australia, coastal Chile, and the southern tip of Africa.

"These are areas where it has wet winters and dry summers," Douggie added. "We studied the deciduous forest biome in school a few weeks ago. I have to say, this is a much more interesting way to learn about these different biomes."

The next grouping of climates the article mentioned was the dry mid-latitude grassland climates. The article listed areas such as the interiors of North America and Eurasia.

"Hey, Mom, where in the world is Eurasia located?" Douggie asked, looking at his globe.

His mother pointed at Europe and moved her finger east towards the area listed as Asia. "Where Europe and Asia meet is generally considered to be Eurasia," His mother explained as best she could.

"Oh, okay. I get it. Thanks, Mom," Douggie said as he gazed at the globe, thinking how cool it would be to visit these areas.

The final category in this grouping was the dry mid-latitude deserts, or Steppes. The article included Eastern Europe, the Gobi Desert and Northern China, as well as parts of Western North America in this catagory. "It says these areas are grassy, but more like a desert in some areas," his mother read. "They typically have very cold winters and warm-to-hot summers."

"I think I remember watching something on the Gobi Desert and the people living there. They ride camels and herd sheep as they move about looking for the best places graze the animals," Douggie added, trying to tie together all the information he and his mother had been gathering. He noticed his journal was filling up quickly.

The final grouping, according to the article, was the high-latitude climates, found from latitudes fifty-five degrees to seventy-five degrees. This grouping included two climates: The Tundra climate and the Boreal Forest climate.

"The article states that both of these are very cold and have long winters and short summers," said Douggie's mother. "Actually, the Tundra regions really don't have a true summer. Also, the temperatures during the winter months will often drop below zero. The rain or precipitation is very low in both climates as well."

"The Boreal Forests are evergreen forests ranging across Northern Eurasia into Siberia," she said. "These forests are also found in Alaska and Canada."

"The Boreal forests take up a huge part of the world," said Douggie, looking at these areas on his globe. "Have you ever been to Canada, Mom?"

"Yes, when I was a teenager. We drove up into Canada during the summer. It was still cool in the evenings and was not very warm during the day."

"One of my pen pals lives in Canada," Douggie said. "That's why he said he misses 'real' summers!" Douggie exclaimed, as if solving a huge riddle.

Douggie's mother nodded at him and returned her gaze to the computer screen. "The last climate is the Tundra, which includes the coldest areas on the planet, she said. "These occur in the arctic regions of the globe near the top and the bottom of the world. The article says these areas never really have true summers and, at its warmest, the temperature only reaches the low forties °F."

"Mom, the warmest day in the Tundra region is colder than most of our winter temperatures here," Douggie stated in amazement.

"I don't think we would enjoy a vacation in those regions," his mother said with a giggle.

"I know, right? No, thank you!"

Once he had finished coloring in his map, Douggie could see where all his pen pals were located and their particular climates. "Mom, did you know I have a pen pal in almost all the major climates of the world? I am only missing two of the climates we learned about, and the areas are fairly simple to find on the map."

"Douggie, do you know what this means?" "What?" Douggie asked.

"We are going to have to find you two more pen pals," his mother stated with a little chuckle.

"I guess so." Douggie responded, as a pained look came across his face.

Questions:

1. What do you think the difference is between climate and weather?
2. Why do you think there are different climates in areas within the same latitudes?
3. Since it takes a great deal of rain to help maintain the rain forest, what do you think would happen if the rain forest were removed?

Vocabulary:

1. Latitude
2. Approximately
3. Deciduous

Chapter 3

HEAVY LEVEES

ESS3-1: Make a claim about the merit
of a design solution that reduces the
impacts of a weather-related hazard.

Douggie's uncle and two cousins were visiting Douggie's family during their summer vacation to California. Douggie had always enjoyed the stories his uncle told about living in New Orleans, especially the ones that included the huge Hurricane Katrina, which flooded their home in August 2005. His youngest cousin, Phil, liked to tell the stories at the dinner table. Douggie had never experienced a natural disaster such as a massive hurricane and the flooding that came with it, but Phil's descriptions made Douggie feel as if he was there in person.

Phil was only seven years old when the hurricane hit New Orleans. The whole town had been preparing for flooding since the levees were designed to handle a hurricane level of three, and Katrina was a level five storm heading right for New Orleans. He described the night it hit and the evacuation that took place, when everyone was trying to get to the Superdome and other places for safety.

"There were large numbers of people trying to get in out of the storm, most confused and panic stricken," Phil explained.

"Several sections of the levee system failed when Katrina slammed into New Orleans, flooding around eighty percent of the town," Douggie's uncle added.

"Some of the houses were flooded for several weeks," Phil said. "Our house was under water for almost three weeks, and we couldn't even get back in to see our house until most of the water was gone."

This story never got old for Douggie. "Were you scared?" Douggie asked his uncle.

"Yes, mostly for my boys. I wanted to make sure we were all safe, with all the commotion and people rushing to get out of town. I was worried I might lose one of them," his uncle explained with a look of concern on his face as memories of the night flashed back into his mind. "I knew we were in trouble when the storm turned into a Category five hurricane, because everyone knew the levees were not in great shape. People kept saying there would be problems if a really large hurricane ever hit our town," Douggie's uncle stated with look of regret on his face.

"Why did it take your town such long to drain after the storm?" Douggie asked the group.

"New Orleans is mostly below sea level, and the levees were built to actually keep the sea out. Without those levees the town would be flooded regularly," Phil answered.

"Why didn't they build a levee that wouldn't break apart when a big storm hit?" Douggie asked.

"They were always working on the levees, but it costs hundreds of millions of dollars to make them more durable, and the government didn't want to spend the additional money," his uncle added. "I think everyone learned an important lesson, and government is working to prevent this from happening again," his uncle continued.

"Hindsight is always perfect 20/20," Douggie's father said as he thought about what Phil had said.

"How does a levee actually work?" Douggie asked the group.

His father jumped in and suggested they look on the internet for the answer to his son's question. His father winked at his brother as if to say, "I've got this one, Bro."

As they searched for information on the design of levees, Douggie was amazed with how simple they really were. One website explained that levees were barriers of earth built up on both sides, with a flat top. The process for construction of a levee seemed simple as well to

Douggie, but he understood it would take time to compact the dirt and rock to keep it from eroding during storm surges.

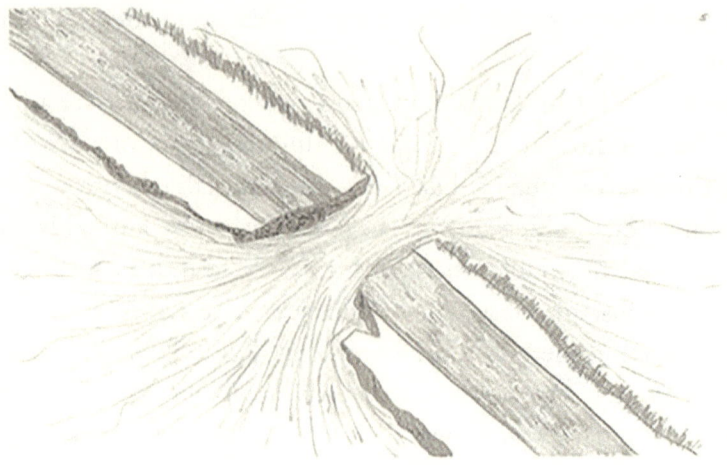

"Dirt alone would wash away too easily," Douggie commented as they read the article.

"Yes, but think about how much money and time it would take to use anything else, like concrete or asphalt," his father responded. "It says here they were still working on the restoration project for the levee system when Katrina hit. They had started the project forty years earlier and it was only supposed to take ten years to finish."

"They took too long fixing the levees, so they were not ready when the hurricane came in and blasted holes in the weakest areas of the levees. The water was able to come in and flood this poor city, including their home," Douggie said, gesturing to his uncle and cousins, sitting at the table playing cards.

"The levees usually do work, Douggie, but they were not all designed to handle the larger hurricanes," Douggie's father explained. "Hurricane Katrina turned out to be one of the most powerful hurricanes ever seen on the planet, much stronger than most storms these levees were designed to protect against."

Douggie and his father continued discussing levees for a few more minutes, then decided to join the rest of the group that was well into a game of "Nerts," the fastest card game Douggie had ever seen. As the group was waiting for everyone to finish shuffling their individual decks, Douggie asked his uncle a question: "Why don't they make the levees taller, wider, and stronger than they are now, you know, to handle larger hurricanes like Katrina?"

His uncle responded without much thought, "They are doing that right now, and they said it would take a decade to finish, but we all think it will take more like two decades."

"You mean they may not be finished upgrading the levees until I am nearly thirty years old?" Douggie asked, checking to make sure he clearly understood what his uncle had said.

"Let's all hope we don't get another Category five hurricane before that time," Phil said, as he finished his last shuffle with a slight look of concern on his face.

Douggie thought for a moment and said, "I think you'd better buy a boat."

After a slight pause, they all started giggling. Soon everyone at the table burst out laughing.

Questions:

1. Why do levees break during storm surges? Explain the problem.
2. Why not make levees capable of withstanding all storms, no matter what size?
3. What is another way to keep the water from flooding a city like New Orleans when a huge storm hits?

Vocabulary:

1. Tidal Surge
2. Evacuation
3. Levee

Chapter 4

THE CYCLE OF LIFE

LS1-1: Develop models to describe that organisms have unique and diverse life cycles but all have in common birth, growth, reproduction, and death.

Yesterday was Douggie's eighth birthday and he had received some very cool gifts. One of his favorites was a terrarium kit. The kit included a base for the water, an area for soil above the water, and a large space above for organisms to live. Douggie decided it would be cool to have a fish or two in the bottom, and some worms living in the soil along with a few plants. The clear dome was tall enough to allow the plant to grow as high as forty-five cm tall. The clear cover allows sunlight through to the plants. The water chamber below needed to be filled originally to a pre-marked line, and more could be added as the soil slowly absorbed a small amount of the water. The water chamber would be fed by moisture runoff from the sides of the dome. The plant would absorb water from the soil, which was moistened from the water below.

"Pretty cool setup," thought Douggie.

Before Douggie could assemble the terrarium, he needed to decide what organisms to put into the terrarium. He and his father went to the pet store to choose a fish for his terrarium. After asking the clerk several questions regarding the fish they had for sale and which ones would live well in the habitat he was building, Douggie decided to go with a Mickey Mouse Platy because they don't grow too large and they reproduce quickly. The clerk actually found one that was pregnant already, which Douggie thought was convenient. Once Douggie had decided on the fish, he asked if they had any worms for sale. The clerk recommended earthworms, but she suggested he use only a few due to the limited amount of soil in his terrarium. He selected two average-sized earth worms to live in the terrarium.

As he and his dad got into the car, Douggie asked, "May we go to the plant place now to get a cool plant for the terrarium?"

His dad smiled and said, "You mean the nursery?"

Douggie smiled and nodded. As they drove to the nursery, Douggie wondered what would be the best type of plant for his terrarium.

His father was also deep in thought regarding the type of plant that would work best in the terrarium. "Douggie we should ask the plant experts which plant they would recommend," his father stated.

Douggie was thinking the same thing. "Okay, Dad, good idea."

The nursery was full of various types of small plants. The worker who was helping them suggested a small flowering plant would work best. A plant that was fast-growing and created plenty of moisture would work best. They chose the mini-African Violet. Douggie decided to grow the plants from seeds instead of purchasing baby plants, because he wanted to see the plants grow from seed to adult and enjoy the whole process. The nursery worker warned them that the plants would take many weeks to flower from seeds.

Douggie didn't mind the wait. "No problem. I'm in no hurry," Douggie responded. The worker smiled at Douggie's dad and nodded, impressed with the young boy's attitude.

With seed packet in hand, Douggie and his father left for home. Douggie started to get excited as he looked at his fish in the bag of water and his packet of seeds.

"Do we have time to build this tonight, Dad?" asked Douggie, with a look meant to inspire a yes from his father.

His father smiled and responded, "There ought to be plenty of time after dinner."

Douggie leaned back in his chair and smiled as he stared at the fish swimming around in the small bag full of water.

After dinner, Douggie and his father cleaned off the dining room table and began constructing the terrarium. The water in the bag from the pet store was almost the right amount to fill the base of the terrarium. His father added some bottled water to fill it all the way to the line. The next step was to add the soil. Douggie's father had a bag of planting soil in the shed, and he asked Douggie to go and bring it in. It took approximately three cups of soil to fill the chamber. A small opening in the center led to the water below.

"This will help maintain a moist soil, but not a soggy one," stated Douggie's father. Douggie took three seeds from his seed packet, placed them in little holes and covered them up with soil. Next, he placed two earthworms on top of the soil and placed the clear dome lid in its place on the terrarium.

He had a perfect place to for his new terrarium on his desk in his room, in front of his window. As long as the shades were open, the terrarium would get sun for most of the day, Douggie decided. "Now comes the waiting," exclaimed Douggie, once everything was in place. Everyone knew this was going to take a while, but Douggie seemed content with waiting and was very pleased to have it in his room. He decided to make a journal entry each day on the progress of his terrarium. Douggie fed the fish daily through a long straw-like feeding tube that ran down into the water below the soil. Next he checked to see if the water was close to the recommended line. When needed, he would add a small amount of water from the water bottle his dad gave him.

Next Douggie focused his attention to the progress of the plants.

At first, the plants weren't doing anything, but soon the little shoots started to appear and his excitement grew. The fish, after a week, actually released its eggs. Very soon the bottom of the terrarium was full of little tiny fish. Douggie's fascination with these little fish made him think about how living things go through life cycles. He started to wonder if there were any similarities between plants and animals, so he decided to keep notes on how both the plant and the animals grew and developed. Each day he added a new set of observations into his journal. At first things were slow and not very interesting, but soon he noticed all kinds of changes taking place in both the plants and the animals.

The small fish became larger and he had to actually remove some and place them in their own aquarium due to a lack of space in the terrarium. The plants began to grow flowers and fill the top of the terrarium. Douggie was excited to have both plants and animals living and growing in his terrarium. Soon, he had to remove the original fish he purchased at the store because it had died. His mom and dad suggested a small funeral and a burial at sea, meaning a flush. The younger fish were doing great and had grown to approximately half the size of their mother. As time passed, Douggie saw a few new shoots forming in the soil; in areas he hadn't planted seeds. Some new seeds must have been dropped by the adult plants, creating new plants. Douggie was starting to see patterns and similarities in both the plants and animals.

Douggie reviewed his notes and began a Venn diagram to show the differences between plants and animals. Next, he filled in the overlapping part in the middle of the diagram with their similarities. To his amazement, there were more similarities than he expected. For instance, they both had a beginning where they were born, they both grew and developed into adults, they reproduce more of their own kind and finally, they both eventually died. Douggie paused, trying to think of any plants or animals that didn't have those four characteristics but none came to mind. "This is the coolest birthday present I have ever received," thought Douggie.

Douggie's mother brought him some modeling clay and asked him to make models of each stage of development of the plants and the animals. Douggie loved modeling clay and was excited about making these models to share with his classmates at school the next day. But it was late and actually past his bedtime. Reluctantly, he went up to brush his teeth and change into his pajamas. His mother took all the clay models and mounted them on plastic plates making it easier to move them around. As she looked at each clay piece she was impressed at how different plants and animals were from one another, yet still shared some basic characteristics.

As she stood there looking at the models she said under her breath, "I think I want one of these. Why does Douggie always get the cool gifts?" She began smiling as she moved into the kitchen to finish the dishes.

Questions:

1. What do the plants provide to the terrarium that helps the animals survive? Explain.
2. Why is it important for most organisms to reproduce quickly in nature?
3. What would be the basic steps in the cycle of all living organisms?

Vocabulary:

1. Terrarium
2. Similarities
3. Reluctantly

Chapter 5

STRENGTH IN NUMBERS

LS2-1: Construct an argument that some animals
form groups that help members survive.

The day had come for Douggie and his parents to visit a wild animal park. Douggie's family had not been there for many years and though his parents said they had taken him before, he had no memory of the visit. His mother downloaded a flyer about the park's recent additions and special exhibits. Douggie was interested in several of the new attractions, including the large elephant habitat and the wolf exhibit. There were other attractions, such as the African Savanna, which had been open for many years that interested Douggie as well. He wished he could go on a real African Safari to see all the native animals, but this park provided a great opportunity to see them as they roamed around in a huge enclosure resembling their natural environment. It was the next best thing to actually being in Africa.

"Douggie, I really can't wait to show you the African Savanna Exhibit. It's my favorite," his mother stated from the front seat.

"I think it will be amazing. I want to see the new Elephant Exhibit as well," stated Douggie.

His dad, not wanting to be left out of the conversation, added, "I'm interested in the Lion Exhibit. Do they get to roam in the African Savanna Exhibit along with the other animals?"

Everyone laughed, knowing he was only kidding.

Douggie, wanting to make sure he had this correct, asked, "They don't let lions in those exhibits because they would kill everything, right, Mom?"

His mother smiled and responded with a quiet nod of her head.

Once inside the park, the map they received at the front entrance showed them a very nice path around the park, ensuring they would see all the exhibits. There was a small train that traveled around the perimeter of the whole park; however, it did not stop at every exhibit. Douggie and his parents wanted to walk and take their time seeing all the exhibits the park had to offer.

The family's first stop was the meerkats, where the little rodent-like animals lived in colonies called gangs or clans. A park ranger stationed near the exhibit provided information explaining how meerkat gangs worked.

The ranger explained how meerkats tunnel in the dirt and assign scouts to keep a lookout for predators. "Once the scout spots trouble, it barks to warn the others," she said. The ranger also told them the meerkats have different jobs; some care for the young, some forage for food, some are the lookouts, and some are the leaders. "They usually are found in groups of twenty or more for protection and division of labor," the park ranger stated, directing the attention of those around listening to the points of interest inside the habitat.

There were signs loaded with information placed around the observation area. Douggie and his parents took turns reading each one. Douggie had his journal with him, along with a small camera his grandmother gave him for his birthday. When they finished at each exhibit, Douggie took a minute to write down a few things he had learned and snap a picture to go in his journal. Douggie was hoping they could discuss his notes later at lunch.

His father smiled at his son. "You getting some good information, Son?"

Without looking up, Douggie answered, "I will show you my notes later at lunch."

Next, they stopped at the rhinos' habitat. These huge animals always interested Douggie. They had huge horns and large bodies with very thick skin, similar to elephants. Douggie was surprised to read that rhinos do not hang out in groups, other than a mother and her calf. The mother takes care of the young calf until it can survive on its own. He learned that the male rhinos are loners and usually do not choose to hang out in groups. Douggie already knew that rhinos are on the endangered species list due to poaching.

Douggie learned that rhinos can stay cool by rolling around in the mud. "Hey, Mom, if it gets hot, can I roll in the mud?" he asked, with a huge smile on his face.

His mom responded, "As long as you hose yourself off before you come into the house." They both giggled. His father was lost in thought wondering how much work it would be to mow all the grass in the enclosure.

As they were leaving the rhino exhibit, Douggie wrote a few things down in his journal and took another picture. "Okay, I am ready to move on," he said after he completed his entry.

The African Savanna was the next exhibit they visited. They saw a huge fence surrounding an area resembling a picture out of a nature magazine. Many kinds of animals shared this enclosure, but Douggie noticed each type of animal typically roamed together in their own groups. The giraffes all stayed fairly close to one another, as did the

Springboks, which looked like deer with white bellies, and the gazelles, which had strange antlers but also looked similar to deer.

"Hey, Mom!" exclaimed Douggie, looking at a big set of information panels about the animals in the exhibit. "See how many different kinds of animals you can find."

Douggie's father took out his binoculars and started looking around the animal enclosure. "I have seen four different species so far."

Douggie kept looking back and forth between the panels and the exhibit. "No fair, Dad, you have binoculars," complained Douggie.

"Yes, but your eyes are better than mine," said his dad, with a smile on his face.

As Douggie continued looking, he noticed when a group of animals was startled they seem to run together in a pack. They all seemed to show the same type of behavior, which was easily observed as a few of the park rangers entered the enclosure driving a golf cart for some reason.

Douggie took down some notes in his journal and noticed he was getting hungry.

"Mom, I'm hungry," Douggie stated, looking up from his writing. "Can we get something to eat soon?"

"Sure," responded his mother, "let's go to the Safari Café, up the hill."

The group gathered up their things and made their way up the hill to the small café.

Douggie was looking forward to sharing his notes from the mornings' adventure and filling his stomach with something tasty. As the group enjoyed their African salads, Douggie shared what he had written in his journal. His dad listened as he ate his salad and studied the map of the park. As Douggie finished sharing his notes, his dad suggested they visit the monkey exhibit and the Animals of the Americas Exhibit.

Douggie mentioned several reptile enclosures he wanted to see. "It says here the pack has alligators, a komodo dragon and an iguana exhibit," read Douggie. They all agreed the lizards were high on the list to see. "We can't miss the elephant exhibit either. It should be amazing," stated Douggie. "It says here they have recently expanded it."

The afternoon grew hot and humid, but the exhibits were interesting and full of fascinating information. Douggie kept filling his journal with new facts from each exhibit despite the heat. His parents, however, were getting tired and quietly wondered when Douggie would run out of steam. They had been walking all day and were ready for a break. Luckily, there was a break area with indoor seating not far from their location. It featured a movie on the American bison and other animals that used to roam free in the grasslands of the Midwestern states. The movie explained what the environment was like for them and how man had hunted them to near extinction. Douggie noticed the bison showed similar grouping behaviors to the other animals he had already seen earlier in the day.

The final exhibit of the day was the elephant enclosure. It was massive – not as big as the African Savanna, but huge. There were twelve elephants of various sizes. There were even three baby elephants. When two park rangers, riding in a golf cart, came into the enclosure, the elephants formed a partial circle around the three young calves, which Douggie thought was amazing.

"Look how they protect those calves by forming a barrier between the young elephants and the golf cart!" exclaimed Douggie.

"I could see where that behavior would be helpful in Africa when lions and other predators tried to attack the herd," added Douggie's father. They all nodded in agreement.

As Douggie finished taking a picture of the elephants and writing down a few notes in his journal, his father offered to get everyone ice cream. The ice cream and the shade of the palm trees provided a welcome relief from the heat of the day.

Since they had finished seeing the attractions on their list and were hot and very tired from all the walking, the family decided to head home. During the two-hour drive home they discussed their favorite exhibits and what information they had learned. A reoccurring theme in Douggie's notes was how animals tend to form groups, mostly for safety reasons.

Douggie's dad thought of a joke and asked, "What is the most important thing to do when being chased by a predator?" Douggie and his mother offered several reasonable answers, but his father rejected them all. Finally his dad answered his own question by saying, "All you have to do is run faster than the person next to you!"

Both Douggie and his mother rolled their eyes and shook their heads, while his dad began chuckling. "At least someone likes his jokes," his mother said, as she looked back at Douggie with a smile.

At home, Douggie had a few things to look up online. He wondered whether animals living in the ocean have similar grouping behaviors for protection. His mother helped him with a few searches, and they found many examples of marine organisms forming groups for protection.

"Douggie, did you know that fish school to protect from predators?" his mother asked, as she read an article online. His dad, overhearing the discussion couldn't resist throwing in a silly comment.

"I thought they schooled to become smarter." Both Douggie and his mother looked at each other and rolled their eyes, but couldn't hold back a smile.

"I remember seeing fish schooling in a few movies," Douggie responded.

Another article describing dolphin behavior explained how they actually hunt in groups. They use sonar blasts to herd fish, such as sardines, toward the surface and then feast on the confused fish.

Douggie took out his journal and wrote down another entry. He had learned a great deal about how animals can protect themselves by staying together in groups. What surprised him the most was how many different types of animals actually formed these groups. He looked at his mother and said, "I guess there really is safety in numbers, usually."

"Unless you're a sardine," his mother added. They both giggled. "Just stay in the middle and keep swimming," Douggie said, as if he were talking to the sardines. They both continued giggling.

Questions:

1. Why was it funny when Douggie's father asked if the lions were allowed in the African Savanna habitat?
2. Why wouldn't lions want to attack the group of elephants protecting their young?
3. Explain one way being in groups can be helpful to fish and one way it may be a problem.

Vocabulary:

1. Savanna
2. Enclosure
3. Predators

Chapter 6

SIMILAR BUT DIFFERENT

LS3-1: Analyze and interpret data to provide
evidence that plants and animals have traits
inherited from parents and that variation of these
traits exists in a group of similar organisms.

Douggie was holding his bearded dragon trying to pet his spiky body. "Mom!" Douggie yelled from upstairs, "Spike is not soft and he is really hard to cuddle with. I think we may need a fluffy, huggable, cuddly dog."

Douggie's mom came into the room where Douggie was holding Spike. "Dogs are a big responsibility, and I'm not sure what your father would say."

"Maybe we can start looking online and see what happens," pleaded Douggie.

"Okay, but no promises right now, you understand?" His mother stated this with a stern voice that left no doubt that she was serious.

"Yes, mother. I understand. We are only looking right now," Douggie repeated with a tone of disappointment.

They decided to start looking at larger dogs first and work their way to the smaller breeds. Douggie had always liked Great Danes, remembering the one his cousins had. "The Great Dane gets incredibly large, I could ride it like a horse," said Douggie.

"They eat more food than our whole family does put together," his mother stated sarcastically.

"Okay, maybe something a bit smaller," Douggie relented. As they searched, one breed became an instant favorite: The Dalmatian. Douggie had liked Dalmatians since he was a very young boy. Hearing stories of them helping firemen and saving people's lives had created a soft spot in Douggie's heart for these beautiful dogs. As they looked at multiple pictures of Dalmatians, Douggie noticed some slight differences; although there was no question they were all Dalmatians and not some other breed.

His mother suggested they continue looking at smaller breeds. "Who knows, there might be another type of dog you like better," his mother stated.

"Okay, but I doubt I will find a dog better than a Dalmatian," Douggie countered.

They searched the internet for more than a half an hour and found all kinds of dog breeds. As his mother had predicted, they found a dog they both liked as much as the Dalmatian.

"Douggie, the Kishu seems like the perfect sized dog. See how noble it looks," his mother added, looking at several pictures of the same breed.

"Look," Douggie added, pointing towards the computer monitor filled with pictures of Kishu dogs. "This one has leopard spots -- and this one is white but not pure white, it has some redness to it."

"Even though they are the same breed, there are differences in color and size," explained his mother.

This statement caused Douggie to think about all animals, and plants. "I remember when Tim's dog Penelope had her puppies. She had six puppies and they all looked slightly different, with various color combinations as well as some differences in their faces," stated Douggie to his mother. "If animals and plants look like their parents, why don't they look exactly like their parents?"

His mother thought that he had asked a good question and suggested they search online for some assistance.

Douggie and his mother soon found an explanation which made sense to them both. They learned that organisms resemble their parents due to the genes that are passed on to their offspring, but there are variations that exist. When both parents' genes are combined, the combinations produce slight differences between the offspring and the parents. Douggie sat back and looked at his mother. "Is this why I look like dad, but not exactly? I have his face mostly, but I have your eyes."

His mother smiled, "Yes, exactly. You are a combination of both your father's genes and my genes," his mother explained.

The website went on to explain how plants, although from the same species, may have small variations or differences in size, color, shapes of fruit, leaves and other plant parts. These variations in plants and animals could potentially have positive effects on the individual organism.

"Mom, that's why Timmy's puppies all looked a different from one another," stated Douggie with a pleased look on his face.

"I think you may be on to something there," his mother replied with a proud look on her face.

"Let's look more into the plant kingdom and see what kinds of differences we can see in the same species," Douggie said with an excited look on his face. His mother wanted to get dinner started, but she agreed to keep looking for a few more minutes.

"What type of plants do you want to look at first, Douggie?" his mother asked.

"Let's look for the vegetables we have in our garden," answered Douggie.

His mother remembered they had planted various kinds of tomatoes and cucumbers, as well as honeydew melon and squash. "This could take a while Douggie, because we have a large variety of veggies out there," his mother warned. "I think we ought to start with the squash. We have three kinds out there. We have zucchini, which doesn't produce until summer. We also planted a few butternut squash, and finally the strange-looking acorn squash."

"Mom," Douggie interrupted, "I already know there are differences in the zucchini we grew last summer. Remember the one that looked like a short sword, the one we thought looked like a football, and the one that looked like a boomerang?"

"Yes, and I was glad to have them back from you intact after I stopped you from playing with them," his mother responded. "I thought you were going to throw the boomerang-shaped zucchini to see if it would come back to you," his mother said with a giggle and a smile on her face.

"Good times," responded Douggie, "good times." The look on his face was one of satisfaction combined with a little regret, because he really had wanted to try out the boomerang zucchini. What surprised Douggie the most about these three zucchinis was they all came from the same plant.

"I think the butternut squash would be a good place to start," Douggie decided, trying to get them back on topic before his mother had to stop the research to make dinner. One site described butternut squash as generally yellow orange in color and cylinder shaped. Douggie knew their squash didn't all match that description. Some were more flat and had a darker orange color, similar to a pumpkin. They were all slightly different from one another.

The final squash on their list was the acorn squash, which everyone in Douggie's family was sorry they had planted because of its strange colors and odd taste. Douggie recalled never getting used to the taste. Most of the ones they had harvested so far were ugly and dark with strange orange blotches.

"The acorn squash all have slightly different color combinations as well as different shapes. They would make better helmets than actual food," Douggie said with a huge smile on his face, hoping to get a laugh.

Playing along, his mother said, "I would be happy to roast one and cut it into the shape of a helmet for you. If it would keep until summer we might be able to use a long zucchini as a sword and an acorn squash as your helmet. What a strange knight you would make. We could call you Sir Veg-a-lot." Tickled with herself, his mother burst into laughter. Douggie smiled, but thinking how cool it would be to really do that.

As Douggie sat and contemplated what they had just learned, he tried to summarize it all in his mind. He figured plants and animals both had members of the same species who were all similar because their traits are passed down from their parents, but within each species slight differences or variations showed up, even between siblings. Douggie wondered what his brother or sister would look like, if he had one. He looked at his mother and asked, "Any chance of getting a little brother or sister sometime soon?"

His mother looked down at him, smiled, and said, "I think I should start dinner now." She quickly got up and walked into the kitchen, hoping Douggie would not want to continue that line of questioning. "Maybe a dog would be a good idea after all," she whispered to herself with a look of dread on her face.

Questions:

1. Why don't you look exactly like your parents? Explain.
2. Some variations you can see, but some you can't. Give examples of each.
3. What would happen if members of the same species had little or no variation? Explain.

Vocabulary:

1. Offspring
2. Variation
3. Boomerang

Chapter 7

NATURE VS. NURTURE

LS3-2: Use evidence to support the explanation
that traits can be influenced by the environment.

Douggie and his mother were on their way to visit Douggie's grandmother, who lived seventy-five minutes away. He and his mother used their time in the car to talk about their visit and different topics that would typically interest his grandmother. His grandmother had a dog she loved dearly, which was one of her favorite topics. Douggie and his mother both agreed that Flower needed more exercise.

"Mom, what is with the name 'Flower?'" Douggie asked with a pained look on his face.

"My mother loves flowers, as you know, so when she got the puppy, it reminded her of flowers somehow and the name stuck. She was one of a litter of four puppies my cousin's dog had a few years ago. My cousin only kept one of the dogs and gave the rest of the puppies away to a few relatives."

Her statement made Douggie wonder why he didn't get one of the puppies from her cousin.

Anticipating his question his mother explained, "We were asked, but your father and I both agreed you were too young and our lives were already difficult with a young boy running around the house. We felt adding a young puppy would make us all too crazy," she explained with a smile on her face.

"Mom, I don't want to have a puppy like Flower. She barks too much and always looks like she is crying."

His mother explained why poodles tend to have browning around the eyes and, with the lighter colored fur, it tends to look more obvious. "With some cleaning, their eyes will look more normal, but it is difficult to keep up with," his mother added.

It turns out that his mother grew up with poodles and had more insight than Douggie expected.

"Well, it looks gross. That's all I was saying," Douggie said with a slightly defensive tone. "I like Flower and all, but she is not like the poodles you see on TV."

"Well, she is a delightful dog and she loves you, as does your grandmother. I suggest you not mention Flower's eyes or anything else your grandmother may find offensive," his mother stated with a serious tone in her voice.

The conversations between Douggie and his mother made the trip feel shorter and they arrived at his grandmother's house faster than Douggie had expected. As they were getting out of the car, the front door of the house opened and two dogs came running out in front of his grandmother. The dogs looked similar because they were both poodles with similar fur color, but one was larger than the other one. Both dogs ran up to Douggie and started licking his legs. He bent down to pet them and they nearly knocked him over with excitement.

"Hello, Dears," his grandmother said as she opened her arms for a hug. Douggie stood up and embraced his grandmother. "My, how you've grown since the last time I saw you, Douggie," his grandmother stated, pinching his cheeks.

Douggie didn't like the pinching, but it made his grandmother smile, so he tolerated it. The dogs were still licking Douggie's legs while he talked with his grandmother, until she sent the dogs back into the house.

"Where did the second dog come from?" asked Douggie as they were walking into the house together.

"I am dog-sitting this weekend for your Aunt Betsy," his grandmother answered. "She got little Peanut from the same litter as Flower came from."

"You mean they are sisters?" Douggie asked with an excited look on his face.

"They sure are," answered his grandmother.

"Why do they look so different?" Douggie asked with a puzzled look on his face.

His mother looked down at Douggie with a very serious look on her face, trying to remind him non-verbally not to offend his grandmother. "Your Aunt Betsy has more time to care for little Peanut and bring her to the pet groomer than I am able to take my little Flower, which causes them to look different from each other," his grandmother explained.

Douggie's mother added, "They are both very cute," trying to redirect the conversation. "Why don't we go into the living room to sit down and talk?"

"Great idea," answered his grandmother. "I have all kinds of amazing pictures to show you from my last vacation in Ireland."

Douggie rolled his eyes. He knew this was going to bore him to death, so he decided to play with the dogs. Peanut and Flower were always ready for someone to play with them, and they got excited when Douggie sat down on the carpet and began petting them. They began jumping around and rolling on the ground, showing their appreciation for his attention.

Douggie was asked to take them outside because of the amont of commotion they were creating. As he took them outside to play fetch, he noticed a few differences between the dogs right away. Peanut, the skinnier one, was faster and got to the ball first most of the time. Douggie also noticed how tired Flower got after just a few minutes of playing fetch. These dogs were not only different in size, but their fitness levels were also different.

His grandmother had said she couldn't get out and walk the dog like she used to, which had contributed to Flower's increase in weight. His grandmother also said Flower loves to eat, and she started putting out plenty of food to encourage her to stop complaining and begging for food. Douggie thought setting extra food out was a mistake, but he didn't want to say anything to be rude.

As Douggie and his mother finished their visit and said their good-byes, Douggie mentioned to his grandmother how he loved the terrarium she gave him for his birthday.

"I knew it was the perfect gift for such a smart little boy as you, Douggie," his grandmother responded, with a look of appreciation on her face. "I hope you enjoyed playing with the dogs today. I know they liked playing with you."

"Yes, we all had a great time. I really gave Flower a great workout." Douggie said with a smile on his face as if he was hinting at something. "Oh good, she needed a good run," his grandmother said, not really paying attention to any type of hinting he may have been attempting.

As they drove home, Douggie started thinking that animals from the same parents can look quite different, depending on the situations they are raised in. He felt his grandmother had been feeding Flower too much food and giving her too little exercise. This had resulted in Flower gaining a great deal of weight. Peanut, on the other hand, was fit and healthy looking.

"I wonder if other animals and plants develop differently when raised in different environments?" Douggie said to himself, under his breath.

"What, Dear?" his mother responded knowing her son was talking but not able to hear what he was saying over the radio.

"Nothing, Mother," he said, looking down at his hands. He really wished he had his journal with him to write down his thoughts.

When he got home, he asked his father for help getting online to research a few topics he had been thinking about on the trip home from his grandmother's.

His dad smiled. "You have a few questions brewing in that head of yours, don't you, Son?" his dad said with a huge smile on his face. "Of course we can get online. We have at least an hour before dinner will be ready. I think I left the computer on, so we don't have to wait for it to boot up," his dad added, curious about what Douggie wanted to research online.

As Douggie explained his observations to his father, some ideas began to develop in his father's mind as to how to search for information. "It sounds like nature versus nurture to me," his dad replied after Douggie had finished asking his questions. "I'm sure we can find a great deal of information on this topic with a few simple searches online."

Douggie's father quickly found a few articles that discussed twins separated at birth and placed in different homes. The articles compared how the twins looked as adults. Douggie thought the pictures were amazing. Some identical twins looked quite different from one another.

Several of the sets of twins had different body weights and other small differences. Some of their hair-dos and even their faces were slightly varied, which Douggie thought might be due to various amounts of sun exposure they had as they were growing up. He remembered his mother discussing sun block and why people need to wear it when they are in the sun to prevent aging of the skin.

Douggie thought for a moment and asked, "Dad, does this mean the traits we get from our parents only partially affect how we look when we become adults?"

"Yes, Douggie, we are all a product of our parent's genes for sure, but we are also a product of our environment," his dad said with pleased look on his face.

"Are plants affected this way to? Do they change with their environment?" Douggie asked, with a puzzled look on his face.

"I think so. Let's look and see if we can find an article explaining how plants can change with their environment."

In a short time, they had found just what they were looking for. The article discussed how a plant's environment can affect its growth and development. Specifically, the articles discussed how the lack of water or proper nutrients in the soil could slow plant growth and keeping them from reaching their potential height. This could also influence the size and shape of their fruit. A stunted tree may produce smaller, shriveled fruit.

"Well, there's your answer, Douggie. Plants can definitely be affected by their environment, much like animals," his dad concluded.

"That's pretty cool," Douggie added.

"Since we have finished our investigation, would you like to go for a run, or an ice cream?" his dad asked, with a huge smile on his face.

"Dad, you already know my answer, ICE CREAM!" Douggie yelled. "Oh, wait, not until after dinner. Your mother would not be happy with me if I gave you ice cream before dinner."

"Not cool, Dad, not cool. You got my hopes up for a minute there," Douggie stated with a look of disappointment on his face, which then turned into a smile.

"Sorry, Son, maybe we can jog to the ice cream shop later," his father said with a chuckle.

Douggie hoped he was kidding as he joined in to his dad's chuckle with a nervous laugh.

Questions:

1. Do puppies from the same litter look identical? Explain.
2. What are some other environmental influences that may cause organisms to end up looking different?
3. Could an environmental change for Flower allow her to looks to change, making her look more like Peanut? Explain.

vocabulary:

1. Embraced
2. Tolerated
3. Nurture

Chapter 8

SCOPING OUT THE PAST WITH FOSSILS

LS4-1: Analyze and interpret data from fossils
to provide evidence of the organisms and the
environments in which they lived long ago.

A traveling fossil exhibit had come to the local community center in Douggie's town. He and his mother had been talking about the fossil exhibit for quite some time, and Douggie was very excited. The day had finally arrived for them to visit the exhibit, and they had decided to walk downtown to the community center, thinking the parking would be a problem. As they reached the community center, their concerns were confirmed. The parking lot was full and cars parked along the neighborhood streets. Douggie's mother was very pleased they had decided to walk.

Once they walked through the door, Douggie saw a sea of people gathered around the different tables or stations. The docent, standing at the door, gave them a brief set of directions and asked them to follow the time progression to each station, starting with the first one to the left, which had a number one on the table. Each station represented a time in history and included a few fossils and a short video discussing the organisms that lived during each particular time period and their environmental conditions.

Douggie couldn't wait to get started. "Come on, Mom, let's go," he said as he pulled his mother's arm toward the first station, entitled "The Precambrian Time." This station covered the time from the beginning over four billion years ago, to 542 million years ago. Douggie and his mother watched the short video which explained that the only life forms during this time were small, single-celled microbes. Douggie then looked through the scope on the table at the fossil bacteria which resembled bubbles trapped in the rock.

"The bubbles are thought to be bacteria and other microbes, the earliest life forms on Earth," his mother said as she read from the small informational packet laying on the table. "The Earth was covered in water and all life was in the oceans and warm, shallow seas."

"Everything was wet, no land at all?" Douggie asked.

"Well, dear, I wasn't there, but both the flier and the video suggest life was in the oceans."

The video described the first life forms as prokaryotic, simple, single-celled organisms. The video continued to describe how cyanobacteria formed and began producing large amounts of oxygen through photosynthesis, changing the atmosphere into one more capable of supporting larger eukaryotic single and multi-cellular organisms.

"Mom, this is cool and all, but I didn't come here to see microscopic bubbles in rocks," Douggie stated looking up at his mother with a pained expression on his face.

"Let's move on then, shall we?" His mother suggested, trying to rekindle the excitement.

The next group of stations had a huge title on a banner hanging on the wall above them which read, "The Paleozoic Era." Each station represented a time period within the Paleozoic Era. The first station they came to was "The Cambrian Period." This time period was 544 million years ago to 505 million years ago and was included in the period of time referred to as the "Age of Invertebrates." Douggie knew invertebrates were animals without backbones.

The video explained that the primary animals in this time period were the trilobites and the brachiopods. Brachiopods still exist today, but trilobites went extinct at the end of the Cretaceous period. The fossils in this station were of a small trilobite and several brachiopod shells embedded in rock.

The video described how brachiopods were marine organisms with valves on the top and bottom and resemble most of sea shells seen today. They started out very small but later, in the Paleozoic era, some grew to enormous sizes. The trilobites lived in virtually every ocean. The video also stated that because of the warm, shallow seas and the availability of plenty of oxygen, an explosion of life forms occurred during this time. In fact, all known phyla showed up during this time. The video referred to it as the "Cambrian Explosion."

"Wow! That is cool. Look at all the kinds of animals living in the ocean during that time," Douggie said as the movie ended.

Realizing the crowds were moving on to the next stations, Douggie and his mother began to move on as well.

The next station was labled "The Ordovician Period." This time period occurred from 505 million years ago to 440 million years ago. This was also part of the age of the invertebrates, although the first animals with backbones showed up during this time as well. The main animal species were trilobites and coral. The fossilized coral at this station were larger and stranger looking than the ones Douggie had seen before. "These resemble the coral I've seen in pictures, although not exactly,"

Douggie said as he closely inspected the fossil remains.

"I guess there have been some changes in the last 400 million years," his mother said jokingly. Douggie looked up and smiled and nodded at his mother.

"Trilobites lived for a long time on Earth, Mom. How did they manage to survive when other species went extinct?" Douggie asked, thinking back to the video.

"The video did say the world was covered by oceans and warm, shallow seas. I guess the environment was perfect for animals such as the trilobites," his mother suggested.

One of the ladies behind them began to crowd towards Douggie and his mother, which encouraged them to go to the next station. The station was labeled "The Silurian Period," the time from 440 million years ago to 410 million years ago. Along with the Devonian Period, the Silurian Period was also part of the "Age of Fishes."

"Mom, it says here that during the Silurian Period the fish ruled the seas and simple land plants began to develop as well. This was followed shortly by land animals, which were the first simple amphibian-like animals."

"The video showed some cool animals. The fish and amphibians were especially interesting to me. They didn't seem to resemble any of the species living now," Douggie stated.

"It would have been an amazing time to live on Earth, but scary, too," his mother added.

To Douggie, the fossilized fish looked similar to the fish he was used to seeing, but more scary looking. "I wouldn't want a fish with teeth coming after me," Douggie stated as he set the fossil back down on the table.

"This thing could probably beat a piranha in a fight," his mother said, smiling down at Douggie. Douggie nodded in agreement as they moved on to the next station.

The "Devonian Period" was the next station for Douggie and his mother. This time period took place between 410 and 360 million years ago. The primary animals were fish, but the amphibian populations were starting to grow durng this time, along with the first ferns and evergreen plants. Land dwelling organisms flourished in the moist, warm environments. With few land animals, the land plants, specifically ferns, began to take over most of the open space.

The station had two fossils. One was a fossilized frond, or leaf of a fern which Douggie found interesting. The other was a fish fossil, which was only a partial picture of the side of a fish head and body. He couldn't pronounce its name, but he thought it looked cool.

"Fish are cool, but I think I prefer the amphibians to the fish," Douggie stated with a very satisfied look on his face.

"Let's go to the next set of stations. They have a sign that reads 'The Age of Amphibians,'" Douggie stated, pointing towards the next few stations.

As they came to the first station in the goup, Douggie said, "There sure are a lot of periods in the Paleozoic Era."

His mother agreed as she started to play the video. The video discussed the first part of the Carboniferous Period: The Mississippian, which took place 360 to 325 million years ago. The video listed the major types of organisms living during this time. The ferns ruled the land and trees with bark started to develop. As for animals, large insects developed in the hot, humid, oxygen-rich environments. Douggie was impressed as the video showed centipedes reaching seven feet in length and dragonflies with wingspans greater than two feet. According to the video the major land animals were the amphibians, and in the oceans sharks began to reign as the top predator. Along with sharks, the seas were filled with all kinds of large invertebrates.

The second part of the Carboniferous Period was the Pennsylvanian, which took place from 325 million years ago to 286 million years ago. The video explained that although this was part of the "Age of Amphibians," the first reptile-like animals had begun to develop.

"Mom, this says the largest amphibians grew to be six feet long, and they dominated the moist swamps, where flying insects had started to develop. Huge dragonflies and cockroaches were everywhere."

"Douggie, I hate cockroaches and bugs now, so I really wouldn't have done well with all those giant insects everywhere."

Douggie laughed, because he knew she was right. He remembered her running out the kitchen in fear after she saw a small cockroach on the floor. These bugs would completely freak her out, he thought.

The video explained how some reptile-like organisms began laying their thick eggs on land during the Pennsylvanian time period. These organisms were the early ancestors of the reptiles and birds. The video also showed how "Pangea," the giant super continent, formed during this time. The environment was mainly hot and humid. Huge swamps had formed at the coastlines as a result of large tidal changes.

Douggie noticed the insect fossils at this station were bigger than insects alive today. The large dragonfly fossil was Douggie's favorite. The rock weighed too much for Douggie to lift, and it had an impression of the largest dragonfly he had ever seen.

"Mom, this is bigger than my head and its not even a complete fossil of the dragonfly!" Douggie exclaimed. His mother nodded in agreement as she ran her hand over the rock, taking in the size and detail of this amazing fossil.

The final station in the Paleozoic Era was the "Permian Period." The video at this station mentioned this era took place from 286 to 248 million years ago. The video showed how the climates were constantly changing. Some parts of the planet were frozen while other parts were hot and dry. Small, egg-laying reptiles became prevalent along with egg-laying mammals. Flies and beetles appear during this time period, as wells as seed-bearing conifers (pine trees), ginkos and cycads.

The fossils in this station included the cross section of a conifer tree, showing rings, and a fossil of a pine cone to go along with it. These fascinated Douggie. The other fossil was the skeleton of a sauropsid, a small egg-laying reptile which is believed to be a possible ancestor to the dinosaurs.

"Mom, this says a mass extinction occurred at the end of the Permian Period where nearly 90 percent of all ocean life, sixty-five percent of the land dwelling animals, mainly reptiles and amphibians, and more than twenty-five percent of the insects went extinct. I wonder what could have changed the climate so quickly?" Douggie stated with a puzzled look on his face.

"I have no idea, but whatever it was, the change was fast and global because it affected most of the species on the planet."

A new set of stations was titled "The Mesozoic Era," and in big letters, "The Age of Reptiles." Douggie was finally getting to the organisms he was most interested in and had come to learn about: The dinosaurs. The first station in the Mesozoic Era was the Triassic Period, which took place between 248 and 213 million years ago. The video for this station showed how the early dinosaurs first appeared, along with small mammals. Other marine organisms also showed up during this time, such as echinoids, which looked like sea-urchins to Douggie. Another looked like a sand dollar he had collected at the beach last summer.

"Mom, these look like sea life we have today," Douggie stated with a surprised look on his face.

His mother agreed as she picked up the stony fossil. "Amazing," she added, with a look of appreciation on her face.

The second period in the Mesozoic Era was "The Jurassic Period," which took place 213 to 145 million years ago. According to the video, this was the best time for dinosaurs. They were everywhere on Earth and ruled supremely. This was also when the first birds appeared.

"Mom, it says here that some scientists believe the birds developed from a group of reptiles that had feathers. Which sounds cool, but I'm not sure what to think."

"We weren't there Douggie, and I have always thought that the fossils were an imcomplete picture of our past anyway," his mother added.

The video went on to explain how pine forests and tropical forest covered much of the land and described how different the environments were at the time. The fossil in this station was a small neck plate from a Stegosaurus. The video showed which neck plate the fossil represented, which was the first of many plates lining the Stegosaurus's back, providing protection from large predators.

Douggie held the fossil up and turned it around in his hands and commented, "Mom, this is the smallest plate. Imagine how huge the largest plates were on this dinosaur! Some must have acted like sails on a windy day."

"It sure is impressive," his mother replied. "No way would we be able to lift one of the large ones. Let's move on to the next station."

The last period in the Mesozoic Era was "The Cretaceous Period," which took place 145 million years ago to sixty-five million years ago. The video for this station mentioned that the dinosaurs were in decline during this time period, however, it was the time when Tyrannosaurus Rex ruled as one of the top predators. Along with the dinosaurs, snakes and various kinds of mammals developed during this time.

The video mentioned that at the end of the Cretaceous Period sixty-five million years ago, another mass extinction took place, possibly due to an asteroid hitting the Earth. The mass extinction resulted in the loss of seventy-five percent of all organisms on the Earth, including the dinosaurs which had ruled Earth for 140 million years. The loss of these giant lizards enabled the small mammals to spread out and take over.

"Douggie, this fact card says this was the first time flowering plants showed up in the fossil record."

"Mom, that isn't why I'm here. Look at the huge fossil of part of a T-Rex arm," Douggie said as he picked up the large bone. "This is massive," he said as he compared it to his own arm. The video showed it to be a small part of the T-Rex right arm. "I think these are my favorite dinosaurs," Douggie mentioned as he handed the bone to his mother. "It's one of the coolest fossils I've ever seen," his mother added.

"Let's check out the next station."

The last two stations were titled "The Cenozoic Era," ranging from sixty-five million years ago to the present.

Douggie looked at his mother sadly, "We are almost done."

"Yes, but we have learned a great deal in just a few minutes," his mother said, trying to be encouraging. "There are also some activities at the end of this exhibit you may enjoy."

Douggie had been fascinated with the stations and he didn't want them to end. "Okay, Mom, let's finish this last period and take a look," he said, with a less than enthusiastic tone in his voice.

This first station was called "The Tertiary Period." It ranged from sixty-five million years ago to 1.8 million years ago and was part of "The Age of Mammals." The video showed how the first horses appeared during this time, although they looked smaller than their modern-day counterparts. Douggie thought they resembled large dogs rather than horses. The fossil shown in this station came from the front leg of an early horse. The video showed where the bone came from on the animal. "Mom, this dog-sized horse was a small animal compared to the horses that are around today."

"That's true, I didn't know they started out the size of a dog," his mother added. "I was also interested in all the types of large mammals that developed during this time," she continued.

"I know, me too. some of my favorite animals showed up during this time. The large cats, whales, elephants, rhinos and mastodons. It would have been cool to live back then," Douggie said.

His mother shook her head and said, "Not for me! I wouldn't want to have to run for my life everywhere I went." They both giggled.

The last station represented the final period in the Cenozoic Era, called "The Quaternary Period," which started 1.8 million years ago. The short video at this station stated how the mastodons, or wooly mammoths, went extinct during this time; however, the modern humans flourished. Scientists know the most about this age because it continues today and scientists can observe many types of organisms firsthand. The video mentioned organisms such as the Dodo bird and other animals which became extinct during this time.

As Douggie watched the video he was amazed to learn how humans have caused many organisms to go extinct by their behaviors. The pollution humans have released into the environment, the removal of large portions of rain forests and the clearing of natural habitats for building homes have been the main contributors.

"It seems we are not only ruling the Earth, but we are damaging it as well," Douggie added with a concerned look on his face.

One of the docents close to their station overheard Douggie and thought he could lighten the mood.

"We are also trying really hard to correct many of the problems we caused by recycling and beach cleanup days, as well as passing laws prohibiting the abuse of the environment."

Douggie felt better and began reflecting on what he had learned from the exibits today. He looked up at his mother with a sheepish smile.

"Can we go through it again?"

His mother's face turned pale white, "Well, uh, look at the time. We need to go and, um, make lunch and I need to do a load of laundry and..."

Douggie interrupted, "I know, I know, we have a schedule. I was kidding." He was actually did want to go back through the exhibit but knew she wouldn't want to take the time. "Maybe I can ask Dad to bring me tomorrow," he said hopefully.

"Well, you can ask him." His mother responded, with a big goofy smile on her face, knowing the answer before he could ask it.

Questions:

1. Why do you think the Precambrian was the longest period of time? Explain.
2. Why is it important to look at the different kinds of fossils in each time period?
3. What information can be gained from looking at fossils from different time periods, particularly about the environment and the climate?

vocabulary:

1. Pangaea
2. Flourished
3. Extinct

Chapter 9

HELP ME VARIATIONS

LS4-2: Use evidence to construct an
explanation for how the variations in
characteristics among individuals of the
same species may provide advantages in
surviving, finding mates, and reproducing.

While Douggie was watching a television nature show on the Galapagos Islands, he heard it mentioned that variation provides strength for the species. Douggie was a little confused and some questions began to form in his mind: "What is variation, and how does it benefit a species? What did they mean by the word strength?"

The video used the plight of the marine iguanas as an example of how variation within a species can be beneficial. The marine iguanas had suffered greatly during an El Niño years ago. The algae, which were their primary source of food, started to die due to an increase in ocean temperatures around the islands, resulting in less food for the iguanas eat. The larger iguanas required a larger daily food intake, and with little to be found, they died first. Some of the smaller males, which required far less food, survived and were able to reproduce, keeping the species alive. In this example, the variation of smaller size was an advantage when less food was available to eat. Although many of the marine iguanas died, the species didn't go extinct, which gave the species, as a whole, strength to survive changes in the environment.

Douggie had several questions come to mind once the video had ended. "Does this same kind of problem occur in plants and animals? Do all species benefit from variation? Where does variation come from?" He decided to write these down in his journal and see if his parents could help him answer them. Since his mother was busy, he went to his father and asked, "Dad, do you have a few minutes to help me research something online?"

"Sure, I have an hour before I have to go to an appointment. Let's fire up the computer and see what we can find."

"Thanks Dad," Douggie said, as he followed his father to the computer.

As they waited for the computer to boot up, Douggie read the questions to his father so he would know where they were headed in their research. Douggie tried to describe the video he had been watching. His father recognized the show as one he had seen before and was able to recall a few of the details. Douggie's descriptions were detailed enough to help fill in the gaps in his father's memory of the video.

They began searching for information online regarding the Galapagos Islands and were able to find several websites filled with information on the marine iguanas and the finches living on several of the islands. One group of finches showed a great deal of variation in beak size. The website described how the size of the seeds that developed on the island each year had a dramatic effect on which finches could survive and reproduce that year.

"Son, it says here the smaller-beaked finches cannot eat the larger seeds, which means the larger-beaked finches survive and reproduce at higher rates than the smaller-beaked finches during those years when the plants only produce larger seeds. Then the next season, a high percentage of the finches have larger beaks. When smaller seeds prevail, the larger-beaked finches cannot handle the smaller seeds as well as the smaller-beaked finches, resulting in the smaller-beaked finches surviving and reproducing at higher rates. The next year a larger percentage of the finches have smaller beaks."

"Dad, this is amazing. You mean to tell me after only one year, the average size of beaks in this population of finches can change?"

"To be specific son, finches' beaks don't actually change over a years' time. Most of the finches with the wrong sized beak die and ones with the correct sizes live and have offspring resembling themselves," his dad said, feeling quite confident in his explanation.

"Okay, that makes sense to me now. What about plants? Do they have variations that can help them survive?"

"Let's see what we can find, Son," his dad answered as he started typing on the computer keyboard again.

"Here is something," Douggie's dad said, not taking his eyes off the computer monitor. "This article addresses plant variations, specifically plant immunity to microbe infection." His father continued to read and summarize the article for Douggie. What they discovered was within the same species of plant, some members of the population are susceptible to infection by a specific type of bacteria, while other members have immunity to the bacteria.

"Wow, does this mean plants can catch a cold?" Douggie asked with a look of confusion on his face.

"Yes, and in this case, they literally can catch a cold and it could result in the infected plant dying," his dad explained.

A second article discussed a few external features of plants which help them survive. "The cactus has several adaptations that help it survive in the desert." Douggie's father read. "A thick outer coating, called a waxy cuticle, helps prevent water loss in the heat of the day. Some cacti have thicker cuticles than other members of the same species, which actually helps them survive better than other members of their species when the weather is at its hottest and driest."

"So, during the worst heat, the cactus with the thickest waxy cuticle has a better chance at survival than a cactus with a thinner cuticle," Douggie summarized, trying to make sure he understood what the article was saying.

"Good job son, I'm impressed with how quickly your are picking up on this."

His father continued his reading. "Spines are another adaptation the cacti have which helps them fend off birds and other animals wanting to make lunch out of their soft inner tissue."

"I tried picking up a cactus before and those spines hurt. I remember my fingers feeling tender for days. I think spines make an excellent defense against predators," Douggie added.

"Well, the website says cactus have varied amounts of these spines, and the ones with the most spines typically have fewer problems with animals eating parts of the plant," his dad stated.

"Nature is so cool," Douggie mentioned, as he started thinking about animals again. His friend Timmy across the street had a few Leopard Geckos that all looked different.

"Timmy's albino gecko looks white and pink, while the other one looks like a normal leopard gecko, tan with dark colored spots. Timmy's mom said the albino gecko wouldn't survive long in the wild because it can't blend in well with its natural surroundings. She said it would get eaten by birds or other preditors faster than you can say breakfast."

"Many animals use camouflage to hide from predators," his father added.

"Timmy's mother was right. Animals with camouflage survive better than ones without it." Douggie concluded.

"It makes sense to me. They would be less likely to be seen by a predator and it may even help them sneak up on their food as well," his father added.

An idea came to Douggie's mind. "I wonder if I could sneak up on the neighbor's cat, Ginger, if I dressed in camouflage? I bet I could make it jump three feet in the air," he thought to himself.

"Hey Dad, do we have any green paint?" Douggie asked, with a huge smile on his face.

Questions:

1. What are some examples of variations in both plants and animals?
2. Using the above answers, how do these variations help the organism survive?
3. Describe some organisms that use camouflage to help them survive?

Vocabulary:

1. Variation
2. Prevail
3. Camouflage

4. Adaptations
5. Susceptible
6. Extinct

Chapter 10

HOME SWEET HOME

LS4-3: Construct an argument with evidence that in a particular habitat some organisms can survive well, some survive less well, and some cannot survive at all.

One day Douggie and Timmy, his neighbor from across the street, started talking about their favorite animals. Timmy said his favorite animal was the Koala. Douggie said his favorite animal was the Emperor Penguin. Timmy liked the cute, cuddly, good-natured little Koalas. He told Douggie the Koalas live in Australia and make their homes in the Eucalyptus trees, eating only specific type of Eucalyptus leaves. Douggie was impressed with Timmy's knowledge of the Koala bears.

"What else do you know about the Koalas?" Douggie asked with interest.

Timmy answered, "I know their baby cubs are born premature and are approximately the size of a jelly bean. I also know that they grow in their mother's pouch, like a kangaroo. My mom got me a book on Koalas a few months ago, and I have read it twice."

"I thought Eucalyptus leaves were poisonous," Douggie stated. "They are for most animals," responded Timmy, "but not the Koala, which really isn't a bear at all." He added, "It got its name because it looks like a teddy bear."

"Timmy, you really know your stuff when it comes to the Koala," Douggie said.

"Thanks! It means a lot coming from you, Douggie," Timmy responded with a big smile on his face. "What do you know about the Emperor Penguin, Douggie?"

"Well," said Douggie, "I know they only live in the Antarctic regions where it is very cold. I also know they are the largest penguin and have special abilities to live in the coldest environments on Earth. They can only lay one egg each season, and the male protects it during the coldest part of the year while the female swims to a slightly warmer location." Douggie added, "Their belly hangs over their feet, where they have placed the egg keeping it warm and protected. I also read they can slow down their body's metabolism to save energy, and they survive huddled with hundreds of other males in a big circle rotating inside to warm up."

The two boys continued their discussion, adding as much information as they could remember about their favorite animals. When they ran out of information to share, Timmy tried to get a rise out of Douggie by stating, "The Koala is able to live in many more environments than the Emperor Penguin."

Douggie, confused by the statement, asked, "Can the Koala live in Antarctica? I think not!" he stated with a look of pride on his face.

"Well, can the Emperor Penguin live in Australia?" Timmy responded, feeling some pride himself.

"No, but there are many animals able to live in Australia, and only a few capable of living in Antarctica," Douggie fired back.

At this, Douggie's mother popped her head in from the other room and said, "Why don't you guys come into the kitchen and get a snack? You both seem hungry to me."

The boys looked at one another, hesitating for a moment before getting up and heading to the kitchen. Douggie's mother had been listening from the other room and thought she could ease the tension between the two boys.

"Both of your animals seem very unique and special. Why don't you each put together a poster about your particular animal and include pictures and facts you have learned? You may want to present your posters to your class once you have finished," Douggie's mother said, showing them a few poster boards she had found in the garage, thinking they would be perfect for their project.

Both boys liked the idea, and after their snack of apple slices and fruit juice, they each chose a poster board and began creating their posters. Douggie's mother printed out some pictures they had selected from online and helped them glue them onto their posters. Since one of the boys' discussion points included their animal's unique habitat, they decided habitats needed to be a part of their posters.

Timmy had a long list of animals that lived in Australia, but a short list of animals capable of eating Eucalyptus leaves like the Koala. Douggie, on the other hand, had a short list of animals that lived in Antarctica but a long list of animals capable of eating fish like the Penguins. When they had finished, the posters were packed with information and pictures of their animals. As they stepped back and looked at the posters, Douggie couldn't help thinking how different these habitats were. Neither animal could survive in the other's habitat.

These animals were perfectly adapted to their particular environments and living any place else would be difficult or even impossible, unless they were in specially created exhibits in zoos.

Douggie began to wonder if plants had the same issues. "Mom, do you think plants have specific habitats they live best in, like animals?" "I don't know. Maybe we ought to look online to see what we can find."

Timmy, knowing where this was headed, thought it was a good time to go see what his mother was doing at home. "I need to go, Douggie. Thanks for all the fun. I'll come back in the morning before school to get my poster. It should be dry by then."

"Okay, thanks for coming over!" Douggie shouted as Timmy rushed out the front door.

"To the computer," Douggie said, as he marched into the front room where the family computer was located.

It didn't take long for Douggie's mother to find a few articles on plants' habitats.

"Douggie, this article on desert plants and their habitats is what we have been looking for. It says desert plants are adapted to dry, hot climates and have specific features which help them survive the harsh environments. They have thick waxy cuticles, or outer coatings, and small or no leaves to help limit water loss. Many other plants have thin cuticles and would dry up quickly in the desert heat."

"If we lived in Arizona, we would need to grow plants with thick cuticles because anything else would probably dry up and die?" Douggie asked.

"Yes, that is basically what the article was stating. I'm sure we could set up a green house with misters to keep other types of plants alive, but out in the heat they couldn't make it. Let's keep looking.

"This next article has information on tropical plants and their special adaptations," his mother stated as she continued to read the article. "It says here tropical plants don't have very thick cuticles, their leaves are large and their stomas are almost always open."

"Mom, what's a stoma?" Douggie asked, interrupting her reading. "I'm not sure yet. Hang on and let me see if they explain later on in the article," she said, trying to be patient but having difficulty. "Oh, here it is," she said. "The stoma is an opening underneath the leaf which allows oxygen, carbon dioxide and water vapor to move into and out of the plant."

Douggie thought for a minute. "I'll bet the stoma in a cactus is usually closed, at least during the day," he stated with a look of satisfaction on his face.

"You may be right, Son. Good deduction."

His mother had only a few minutes left before she needed to start dinner, and she was starting to get anxious. "Is this what you wanted to know, Douggie?" she asked hoping he would be satisfied.

"I think so, Mom," Douggie responded. "I see why the tropical plants don't grow in the desert. It's because they need a great deal of water in the air and rain to replace the water they lose during the day through their open stomas. They would dry up to a shriveled little twig if they were in the desert."

Douggie went to get his journal and write down what he had learned. Organisms live in habitats best suited for their adaptations. If the organism is placed in a habitat other than their natural one, they may have trouble finding food and shelter. Some organisms can live in habitats other than their own, but life there would be very difficult for them. Also, organisms simply can't live in all habitats. Some habitats are either too cold or hot for all organisms to live in.

"Our Earth is an amazing place," Douggie said to himself. "There is such a variety of organisms and habitats. I wonder if Mom and Dad wouldn't mind taking me to all the habitats on Earth?" he said with a smile on his face. "I think I will wait to ask until after dinner."

Questions:

1. If you were to have to choose between the Koala or the Emperor penguin for a pet, which would you prefer? Explain why?
2. Of the two animals, which is the most specialized for their particular environment? Explain.
3. Of the types of plants, which one do you think would be able to live in the largest number of habitats?

Vocabulary:

1. Unique
2. Adapted
3. Habitats
4. Premature

Chapter 11

VACATION WITH FOXES

LS4-4: Make a claim about the merit of
a solution to a problem caused when the
environment changes and the types of plants
and animals that live there may change.

Douggie was excited when his dad gave him the news. His architectural company had given their family a cruise around the Channel Islands and a three-day stay on the Island of Santa Catalina. It included a day trip to Santa Cruz Island, where they could enjoy beautiful hiking trails and other fun activities including snorkeling and kayaking.

"When do we get to go?" Douggie asked with his usual enthusiasm. "In two weeks, during our spring break," his father responded.

"It should be a great time," his mother added, as she was cleaning off the table for dinner.

"I want to learn as much as possible about these islands to help us get the most out of our visit," said Douggie excitedly.

"Remember, we are only going to be on two of the islands, Santa Cruz and Santa Catalina," his dad said for clarification.

"Okay, so I will limit my research to those two Islands," Douggie responded. "Do you think we can get online now?" Douggie asked.

"Not before dinner," his mother responded. "It's nearly ready. Please go wash up and come to the table."

After dinner, Douggie and his father looked online for specific activities they could do during their visit on each of the islands. Catalina Island had plenty of activities to enjoy and beaches to visit. They looked up the hotel they were staying at and discovered it had a pool and several interesting shops and restaurants nearby.

Their excitement really grew when they looked up the Island of Santa Cruz. They learned that Santa Cruz was a very large island, with areas owned by the National Parks Service (NPS) and an even larger part owned and operated by The Nature Conservancy (TNC).

"This island alone will make this a great trip," Douggie stated to his father. "I can't wait to talk to the rangers and ask them questions about the various types of plants and animals that live on this island."

His father smiled, thinking about the poor rangers and all the questions they were going to have to answer. "I'm sure they will enjoy the opportunity to share what they do and answer all your questions," his father added, trying not to smile.

"Let's keep reading, Dad. Maybe we can find some interesting facts about the history of this island," Douggie said excitedly to his father.

As they continued their search, one animal and its plight came up multiple times: The Sana Cruz Island Fox. As his father read the article aloud, Douggie was hoping this would be an amazing story. He wasn't disappointed. The article explained how the Santa Cruz Island Fox had lived on the island for thousands of years as the top predator. Then, because of humans using a pesticide called DDT, the population of Bald Eagles declined drastically. Humans also brought sheep, pigs and cattle to the island, resulting in a loss of the vegetation which provided cover for the fox to hide in.

Lastly, the Golden Eagles started nesting on the island, taking up residence because of their love of feral pigs for dinner and the unfortunate lack of Bald Eagles to keep them away. The Golden Eagles started preying on the little island fox because they were easy to see and catch, resulting in a dramatic drop in populations of the Island Fox in the 1990s.

"Dad, I can't believe this started happening because of us using DDT, causing the Bald Eagle to die off," Douggie said as his dad continued reading.

"The Island Fox wasn't used to flying predators and became easy prey for these large birds. The populations of these small cat-sized foxes had dropped from around 1,500 to fewer than 100 by 2003. The Nature Conservancy, the National Parks Service, and the Department of Fish and Game came up with a plan to save the Island Fox from extinction," his father read.

The article explained their detailed plan for getting rid of the grazing animals, the feral pigs and even the Golden Eagles.

"I'm glad they decided to do something, but they were almost too late," Douggie reasoned.

His father nodded in agreement, "I know. The Island Fox was on its way out for sure, with their numbers below 100."

His father continued reading the article aloud to Douggie. The group had decided to hunt down the pigs using a variety of methods intent on completely eliminating them from the island instead of transporting the pigs somewhere else. The reason they decided on killing them was because pigs were listed as pests. The pig population could not simply be controlled on the island due to their high rate of reproduction and would quickly overpopulate the island again. The group had already successfully removed the sheep and other grazing animals a few years earlier without killing them and some people were having trouble with the idea of killing all those pigs. Though unpopular with many, the plan was carried out anyway.

"Dad, I can see why people wouldn't want to kill all those pigs, but I guess this was the fastest and easiest way to get them off the island."

"No doubt, and the article said the pig farmers were not interested in the feral pigs due to diseases they could be carrying."

According to the article, the next part of the plan was to reintroduce populations of Bald Eagles, which would run off the Golden Eagles from the island. Unlike the golden eagles, the bald eagles don't feed on island foxes which became an important step in helping the island fox populations increase. They also captured and released the remaining golden eagles back onto the mainland. With the golden eagle population down to zero, they were one step closer to helping the island foxes return from the brink of extinction.

"I am amazed at the complexity of this plan," his father stated. "These people really had it all together," Douggie added with a look of appreciation on his face.

Captive breeding, the article stated, was a key component in the rescue of the island fox. They would temporarily hold pairs of foxes in enclosures resembling their natural habitat, encouraging them to breed and reproduce offspring. They would release them back on the island, giving their numbers a boost. The group managed to release close to eighty fox pups in just a few years.

"Wow, that's like doubling their number," Douggie stated.

"This program really seems to be working," added his father. "The article called it the most successful rescue of any endangered species ever. By 2013, there were approximately 1,500 island foxes on Santa Cruz. They will soon be removed from the endangered species list."

"No way! That's amazing," Douggie added, raising his arms in celebration. "I can't believe this worked so well. I couldn't be happier for the Island Fox," Douggie stated with a huge smile on his face.

As the two sat back in their seats, trying to take in what they had just learned, Douggie started thinking about all the things people had to do to help save the foxes. "Dad, I wish they hadn't shot and killed all those pigs. It wasn't their fault they were there," Douggie stated with a small look of regret on his face.

"Well, Son, the article said the pigs were listed as pests," Douggie's dad answered. "They couldn't capture them and release them in the wild on the mainland. That would be against the law."

"Couldn't they have shipped them to a pig farm and at least let them live as domestic pigs?" Douggie asked, hoping he had found a reasonable alternative to killing them.

"I don't think the farmers wanted the feral pigs. They could have brought in diseases and other things to make their own pigs sick," his father added.

"I guess the only thing they could have done was hunt them down and kill them. It is unfortunate but I am really happy it helped save the foxes. The hunters must have been able to stock up on all kinds of pig meat, so I guess it was worth it to them and pigs were not wasted," Douggie concluded.

"What's for breakfast in the morning, Mom?" Douggie yelled to his mother in the kitchen.

"Bacon and eggs, why do you ask?" his mother answered.

"Just curious," Douggie responded as both he and his father looked at one another and chuckled quietly.

Questions:

1. Why do you think the Island Foxes were easy prey for the golden eagles?
2. Explain the basic reason the golden eagle was on the island in the first place.
3. Why do scientists consider the rescue of the Island Foxes one of the most successful rescues ever?

Vocabulary:

1. Pesticide
2. Endangered
3. Feral
4. Alternative
5. Overpopulate

Chapter 12

TUG AND SHOOT

PS2-1: Plan and conduct an investigation to
provide evidence of the effects of balanced and
unbalanced forces on the motion of an object.

Douggie's third-grade class was competing against the other third grade class for the right to use the soccer field during the next two weeks. The classes have been arguing lately about which class gets to use the field during recess, and the teachers agreed a contest would help them decide. They choose a competition of tug-a-war. The winning team earns the right to use the field for the next two weeks, and the other class gets the field for the following two weeks. This had become a matter of pride for both classes and they were both determined to win. Each class selected ten kids to compete in the competition, and the rest of the classmates got to cheer for their own team.

The teachers created three lines on the field: The center line where the flag started, and two end lines ten meters from the center line on either side. The object of this game was to pull on the rope and make the flag cross your own end line. Both teams were ready, some with paint under their eyes like football players use. Douggie assumed it was used to intimidate the other team. Douggie was in the crowd, cheering for his class.

When the teacher blew her whistle, starting the game, both teams pulled with all their strength. Douggie positioned himself in the middle in order to see the flag and watch its movement. To his amazement, the flag didn't move. It stayed right on the center line. Both teams' faces were straining, and yet no movement occurred. This made Douggie start questioning why there was no movement when a great deal of force was being used by both teams. He almost forgot to cheer but the noise from the crowd brought his thoughts back into the moment and he rejoined his classmates as they tried to encourage their team to pull harder.

After what seemed like five minutes of intense pulling, but actually was only two minutes, both teams started moaning and groaning in pain. One student yelled, "My arms hurt. Can we stop now?" The teachers started giggling.

"Another student yelled, "I can't go on. My arms are going to fall off!"

One student in Douggie's class said, "I think I'm going to pass out," which was an obvious ploy to gain sympathy from two quite unsympathetic teachers.

One student, trying to be funny, yelled, "I have to pee!" At this, everyone started laughing. The laughter grew and grew into a huge, uncontrollable, hilarious laughing session. Kids were laughing so hard they were almost crying. Both teams lost control of the rope and fell to the ground laughing and in obvious pain. While the teachers were busy helping the students up off the grass and making sure everyone was okay, Douggie's thoughts returned to his question about why the flag never moved. He thought one of the groups would be able to pull hard enough to move the flag in one direction or the other, but it was a tie. The flag never made it off the center line.

The teachers were faced with a dilemma. They had to design a different contest to break the tie. They decided to use penalty shots at the soccer goal, which had a goalie from the other team trying to defend the goal. The teachers agreed that since they were competing to play on the soccer field, this would be an appropriate test. The kids agreed and went about choosing a new set of players for each team. This time everyone but the two players, the goalie and the person shooting the soccer ball, were sitting outside the penalty area on the grass, watching. Each team would get five shots, alternating teams between each shot. Each class picked three boys and two girls to shoot the goals.

Douggie got picked this time because his classmates thought he was one of the best shooters in the class. Truth be told, Douggie fancied himself more as a defender than a striker, but he wanted to play, so he kept his thoughts to himself. Douggie was in line to shoot second for his team.

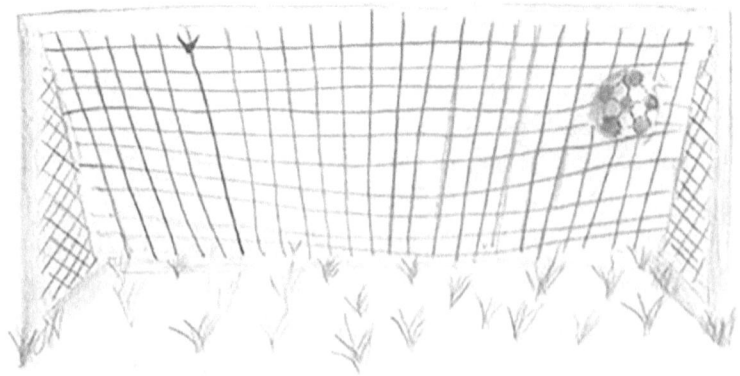

The first player from the other team shot and scored, but everyone knew he was going to make it because he was the best soccer player in the third grade. For Douggie's team the first player to shoot was Timmy, Douggie's neighbor from across the street. He kicked the ball very hard, but it hit the goal post and bounced off. The goal post kept rocking for some time after the kick.

Douggie knew Timmy would be upset, so he got up and put his arm around Timmy's shoulder and said, "Good try, Timbo. We still have four more shots, and by the way, you kicked it so hard the goal post is still rocking." At this, Timmy forced a small smile and sat down.

The second player for the other class got up and set the ball on the mark. He looked right at the goalie, for a few seconds. A hush came over the crowd of students as they waited for him to kick the ball. As he started running towards the ball he lost his footing and stumbled slightly, which threw off his aim and he kicked the grass behind the ball. Once his foot actually hit the ball, there wasn't much power left and it rolled slowly to the goalie. A sense of relief came over Douggie's team now that they had a chance to even the score.

It was Douggie's turn to shoot. He got up off the grass, grabbed the ball, placed it on the mark and backed up. As soon as he had reached a reasonable distance from the ball, he started running up to kick the ball. With one big kick the ball sailed into the right upper corner of the goal. The score was tied, and his whole team cheered. A feeling of delight came over Douggie as he walked back to his spot next to Timmy. In the next few minutes the teams were able to decide on a clear winner. Douggie's team lost the competition by one point. As they were walking back to their class, Douggie noticed his foot was a little sore from the kick. "I kicked the ball. Now why is my foot sore?" Douggie said to himself. Actually, he had several questions regarding today's activities. In class, Douggie raised his hand. But before he could say a word, Douggie's teacher said, "If you have any questions, please write them down in your journal for us to address later, after you read." Douggie did as he was asked, and wrote his questions in his journal. He really wanted to ask his teacher the questions, but he knew there probably wasn't enough time before the bell was going to ring for them to go home.

Sure enough, before the class had finished reading the assignment, the bell rang, indicating the end of school. His teacher excused them to line up and make their way to the front of the school for pick up.

"Douggie, I'm sorry we didn't get to your question. Maybe we can address it tomorrow," his teacher said with a smile on her face. Douggie didn't want to wait that long and hoped his parents could help him with this little dilemma.

When he got home, Douggie showed his mother his journal, including the questions he had written down, and told her all about the games his class had played that day. The first question was, "Why does something not move, even though there are people pulling on it from both directions?" The second question was, "Why did my foot hurt after I kicked the ball?" The last question was, "Why did the goal post shake after it was hit by the ball?"

"Well, I'm not sure," his mother said. "We will need to look online to see if we can find the answer," she added, motioning to the computer, which was already on and ready for them to use. His mother quickly found a website explaining forces and motion. As she read the article to Douggie, they both learned about the laws of motion, describing why things either move or don't move when force is applied to an object.

"Hey, this explains why the flag didn't move," Douggie said. "It takes unbalanced force to change the motion of an object."

His mother added, "It's Newton's First Law of Motion: Objects in motion or at rest stay that way until an unbalanced force is applied to the object."

"Does this mean both teams were applying the same amount of force, but in opposite directions?"

"Yes, which must have created balanced forces on the rope, keeping the flag from moving."

"This makes sense to me now," he stated with a look of satisfaction on his face.

"What about the soccer ball?" Douggie added, wanting to get the whole picture. "Well, do you think the force you applied to the ball was balanced or unbalanced?" his mother asked, knowing he would get this one.

"The force was an unbalanced force and that's why the ball moved!" Douggie exclaimed. "But why did my foot hurt?"

His mother smiled. "Why don't we keep looking at these laws of motion and see if they can help."

As they continued their search, Newton's Third Law provided an explanation. "It says here that when forces are applied to an object, there are always two forces acting. With every force applied, there is another force applied back in the opposite direction that equals the applied force," his mother read.

Douggie, trying to summarize, said, "My foot applied a force to the ball and the ball applied a force back on my foot, that's why it was sore after I kicked it."

"Sounds right to me," his mother responded. "I guess you kicked it too hard," she said trying to tease him a little.

Douggie looked at his mother, trying to figure out if she was serious. "Mom, I had to score. I couldn't let my team down," he said with a very serious look on his face.

"Well, it wasn't the 'World Cup' or anything. It was just a silly game," his mother said, again trying to tease him.

At this he realized his mother was teasing him and said, "Well, to me it was as important as the 'World Cup.'" A little smile developed on his face.

His mother smiled at him, gave him a big hug and said, "Way to go, my little Messi."

Questions:

1. If the teams had not had the same number of players, would it still be possible to have the same result? Explain.
2. If two people pushed on a stationary object with the same amount of force but in opposite directions, would the object move? Explain.
3. When Douggie kicked the ball, was the force applied to the ball balanced or unbalanced? Explain.

Vocabulary:

1. Dilemma
2. Amazement
3. Opposite

Chapter 13

THE CRADLE

PS2-2: Make observations and/or measurements
of an object's motion to provide evidence that a
pattern can be used to predict future motion.

Douggie's father was on a business trip to New York for five days.
He promised to bring Douggie a gift when he returned from his trip.
Douggie waited anxiously for his father's return. When his father got
home, after all the hugs and kisses, he gave Douggie a box and asked
him to open it. Inside was a frame holding five small steel balls, each
suspended by two strings. "It's a Newton's Cradle," his father stated.

"I have seen this before," Douggie responded. "I've always wanted
one of these. Thanks, Dad!"

"I'm glad you like it," his father said, smiling at Douggie's mother.

Douggie took the mechanism with him and sat at the kitchen table
to try it out. The first thing he did was pull one ball back and let it
slam into the other four. When it did, four stayed still but the last one
in line, on the opposite side from the one he dropped, swung upwards.
When it came back down, it hit the other four, and the original ball he
had dropped swung back upwards.

"This is so cool," Douggie exclaimed as he watched the motion continue. Next he tried dropping two of the steel balls at the same time to see what would happen. When the two balls hit the remaining three, three stayed still, and the two on the opposite end from where his hit flew upwards.

Douggie started to see patterns developing and thought this would make for a great investigation. "Dad, this is amazing. I'm going to figure this all out," he stated with a look of determination on his face.

"I'm sure you will, my son, I'm sure you will."

Douggie went up to get the new journal his mother had purchased for him since he had filled up his last one. This journal was blue, his favorite color. In it, Douggie decided to place a small chart to keep track of each trial with the mechanism. In the chart he started by making a column for the amount of steel balls dropped at the beginning. The next column was for his prediction of how many would move after the impact. The last column was for the actual number of steel balls Douggie observed moving upward after the initial impact. Since there were only five steel balls in total, he listed one through four in the first column.

Things were easy until he reached three at a time. When he dropped three at a time, they hit the remaining two but what happened next was surprising to Douggie. Three swung upwards and the last two of the group he had dropped, stopped. When the others swung back and hit the two that were stopped, three swung upwards again and the original two on the other side completely stopped again.

"That was amazing," Douggie exclaimed. "I didn't expect that to happen at all. I wonder what would happen if I dropped four at one time?" In his journal, Douggie made his prediction and released the four balls towards the single, motionless ball. When they collided, four went flying upwards, and one single ball remained behind. When they came back down and collided, the same thing happened. Four flew upwards and one stopped. This motion kept going, but Douggie noticed that each time the balls flew up after the collision; they didn't go quite as high as the previous time. This continued until the balls slowly came to a stop.

Once Douggie had finished with four at a time, he decided to try one from each side and drop them at the same time. In his chart he made his prediction and carried out the experiment. To his amazement, they hit and both bounced right back upwards close to where they had started. Next, he released two at a time next and watched. When two were dropped from each side, those same two bounced back upwards towards where they had begun, and the one left in the middle didn't move at all.

Something about these investigations left him curious. He noticed all the balls eventually came to a stopping point. With each collision, the balls lost some of their motion until they eventually stopped. Douggie wondered what was causing the balls to slow down so fast. In his opinion, they ought to keep going for quite a long time, but it wasn't even close to what he observed.

Douggie went to ask his father for help with his question. His father was on the couch reading some newspapers that had collected while he was gone.

"Dad, I have a question. Why do the steel balls eventually come to a stop? No matter what I do or what combination I use, they always end up stopping. What is stopping them?" Douggie asked with a curious look on his face.

"Well, I think I know but I'm not positive. I'm sure I know where to look for the answer though," his dad responded, getting up from the couch as he was talking. "I will start up the computer and together we will see if we can find an explanation of this strange result." Douggie was pleased his father was ready to help so quickly, and he followed his father to the computer holding his Newton's cradle.

"Dad, do you think there is something taking energy out of the steel balls when they collide?"

"It makes sense to me, but what do you think could cause this to happen?" his father asked.

"I know friction can slow stuff down, but these balls barely touch, so how could friction be an issue?" Douggie responded thoughtfully.

As they looked online, one website provided a simple explanation. The steel balls were transferring part of their kinetic energy into the air around them. This transfer of energy was in the form of friction called air resistance. The tiny air particles were hitting the steel balls as they move through the air and, little by little, slowing them down.

"Dad, this explains why the wind pushes on my hand when I stick it out the car window while we are moving, right?" Douggie asked, feeling confident he already knew the answer.

"Yes, I think you have it, Douggie," his father responded.

"I think air resistance affects anything moving through the air," Douggie said.

"Didn't you and mother look up Newton's laws the other day?" His father asked, trying to get him to remember the first law.

"I remember objects in motion stay in motion unless an unbalanced force affects them," Douggie stated as best he could from memory.

"Very good," his father responded with a big smile on his face. "What was the unbalanced force causing the steel balls to eventually stop moving?"

"I guess the air resistance is the unbalanced force we were looking for," Douggie answered.

"Now I know why they call this Newton's Cradle. This thing shows us how to apply Newton's laws," Douggie said with a huge smile on his face.

As he and his father were looking at other related websites, Douggie forgot he was holding the cradle in his hands and the strings became tangled. His father looked down at the now tangled mess and said, "You know, this apparatus can teach us more than I thought, like figuring out how to untangle things," he said with a chuckle.

Douggie looked down at his mess and said, "I think I'm going to need some help with this, Dad." His father looked down at his son fussing with the tangled mess and decided to help him get it all untangled.

"Why couldn't I have given you a simple toy car or something?" his father said with a smile on his face.

"Dad, you know I would have found a way to use it in some other kind of investigation," Douggie responded. They both began to chuckle because they knew it was true.

Questions:

1. Why do you think the same number of steel balls as were dropped flew upwards after the collision? For instance, when one ball is dropped, only one ball from the rest flies upwards. When two are dropped, two will fly upwards from the rest.
2. Would the steel balls come to rest faster if they weighed more?
3. Why do all the steel balls have to be the same weight?

Vocabulary:

1. Mechanism
2. Swung
3. Apparatus
4. Unbalanced force
5. Anxiously

Chapter 14

MAGNETIC POSSIBILITIES

-3: Ask questions to determine cause and effect
relationships of electric or magnetic interactions
between two objects not in contact with each other.

The special day had arrived. Douggie and his parents had planned
a trip to the local science center. It was one of Douggie's favorite places
to visit because of all the cool activities and interesting exhibits. They
had found that most of the people working there were very helpful
and usually had helpful answers to their various questions. Douggie
remembered one docent who was especially helpful and informative.
His name was Alfred. He also had a cool accent and loved to talk to
kids. Douggie and his parents had tried to go the Science Center at least
once every month. They had purchased a season pass a few years ago
and had such a great time, they continued renewing their membership.
Douggie always enjoyed looking at all the new exhibits they created
each month. This month's new additions included a series of magnetic
activities and static electricity observations. They also had a new short
film on Nicola Tesla. Douggie was looking forward to visiting these
new exhibits as well as some of his favorites.

Once they had arrived and entered the center, Douggie picked
up a brochure and a map of all the exhibits including the new ones.
Douggie decided to go to the "Magnetic Experience" first. This exhibit
had hands-on activities including electromagnets, some permanent bar
magnets and a whole section devoted to static electricity. At the table

with the electromagnets, Douggie saw a wire wrapped around a small four inch long metal rod. The two ends of the wire were connected to a large battery.

Douggie picked up the metal rod and touched a pile of paper clips. The magnet managed to pick up more than 15 paper clips. Douggie was amazed. At that moment a docent reached over and unhooked one of the wires connected to the battery, and all the paper clips fell to the table. Douggie, again, was amazed.

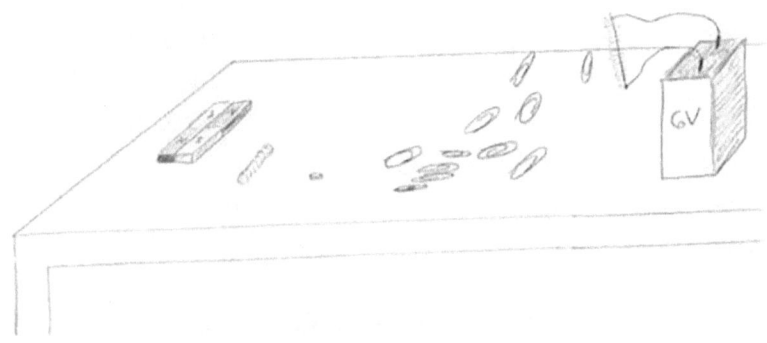

"That's so cool!" Douggie exclaimed.

"Aye, Laddie, that it is," came a voice from behind him. Douggie turned around and saw his old friend Alfred.

"Glad to see you, Alfred," Douggie said with a big smile on his face. "I was wondering if you were working here today."

"That I am," Alfred confirmed. "Enjoying our new activities, are ye?" Alfred asked Douggie.

"I sure am," Douggie responded.

Alfred showed Douggie the three different electromagnets and asked him to use each one to pick up paper clips. The second electromagnet had twice as many coils of wire around the center iron bar as the first one he had used. This second magnet picked up 28 paper clips. "Wow, that's almost twice as many paper clips as the first magnet," Douggie exclaimed.

"Aye, Laddie, now try the last magnet. It only has half as many coils as the first magnet. Can you predict how many paper clips it will pick up?"

"I guess it would be about half as many as I picked up on the first one," Douggie responded, not really sure of his answer.

As Douggie picked up the last magnet and placed it in the pile of paper clips, Douggie felt a hint of anticipation. Would he be right? He would soon find out. As Douggie lifted the paper clips out of the pile and set them down to count, he knew there were not as many this time. He counted only nine paper clips, confirming his hypothesis.

"I was right, mostly," Douggie said as he finished counting the paper clips.

"Well done, Douggie," Alfred stated as he placed the paper clips back into their pile. "I am quite impressed."

"What about those other magnets? Are they fun to use, too?" Douggie asked Alfred, who was already moving toward the table with the permanent magnets on it.

"Aye, they have some interesting properties which make them behave differently than the electromagnets. For instance, these permanent bar magnets have a north and a south end to them. If you were to try to connect two north ends or two south ends together you would see a completely different response than if you connected one south end to one north end together. Go ahead and give it a try, Laddie."

As Douggie started his investigation, he tried to remember concepts he had learned about magnets. He remembered they usually attract one another, but sometimes they actually push each other away, or repel. Douggie couldn't remember when they attracted and when they repelled, so he made this the focus of his testing. In the first trial, Douggie tried to connect two north-pole ends, thinking they would attract. He found out they actually repel one another.

For his next trial Douggie tried connecting two south-poles. He predicted they would repel much like the two north-poles did. When he tried to connect them they repelled, exactly as he thought they would.

"Cool," Douggie said as he finished his second trial.

For the final trial, Douggie tried to connect the south-pole end with the north-pole end of the magnet. He predicted they would attract this time. As he brought the magnets close, they pulled together and held tightly.

"I was right!" Douggie exclaimed with a smile on his face. "Good job, Honey," Douggie's mother said from behind him.

"Let's try something else," Douggie stated, his excitement growing. "Why don't you try using the bar magnets to pick up paper clips?"

Alfred said, pointing to the other end of the table and a pile of paper clips.

Douggie made his way to the pile of paper clips with three bar magnets to test. For the first trial, Douggie used one magnet to see how many he could pick up. He made no prediction because he had no idea how many he would get. When he pulled up the magnet from the pile of paper clips, he counted six paper clips attached to the magnet.

"I'm going to try two magnets together this time," stated Douggie. "How many paper clips do ye think you will get this time?" asked Alfred looking over Douggie's right shoulder.

"I think I will pick up twice as many, or twelve," Douggie responded. "Give it a try, Laddie," Alfred said. By now, a small crowd was gathering around the table watching Douggie complete his experiments. As Douggie pulled out the two magnets from the pile of paper clips, he smiled. Douggie counted 13 paper clips attached to the two magnets. "Wow, this is so awesome!" Douggie exclaimed. "Let's try three this time. I wonder if they will pick up 20 or more paper clips."

As he placed the three magnets together, Douggie noticed other people gathered around to see the demonstration, including a few younger children. As he lifted up the magnets from the pile of paper clips he noticed he didn't see as many paper clips hanging onto the magnets as he thought there ought to have been. When he finished counting, there were only 17 paper clips.

"What happened this time?" Douggie asked with a look of frustration on his face. "Why didn't we get more like twenty paper clips?"

Alfred answered his question with a question. "Why do ye think we had different numbers than what we predicted?"

"Maybe the magnets are different strength or something," Douggie responded.

"Sounds good to me," Alfred said with a smile. "How could we test them to determine if the magnets are the same strength?" Alfred continued.

Douggie thought for a moment and answered, "If I tested each magnet individually and counted the number of paper clips each one picked up on their own, I would know if they were the same strength or not."

"Well done, Laddie," Alfred stated with a smile on his face.

"Why don't we go see the static electricity center," suggested Douggie's father, trying to let other people have an opportunity to use the demonstrations at the table.

As they made their way to the next center, Douggie was wondering what they would have for him to experiment with. His parents followed behind, letting him find his own way. Alfred was talking with some of the other children at the bar magnet center, and totally enjoying the experience as much as the kids were.

The static electricity center had one object that looked like it had come out of a science fiction movie. It was called a Van de Graff generator. As Douggie approached the machine, he saw a young girl with long hair put both her hands on the metal ball at the top of the machine. What happened next amazed him. The girl's hair started standing on end in all directions. It reminded him of the cartoons showing someone getting electrocuted, with their hair frizzed out.

A docent was standing next to the girl explaining how the machine worked as Douggie approached. "The metal ball was building up a positive charge on its surface, and when she touched the metal surface, a similar charge began building up on her body, even to the ends of her hair. Since like charges repel each other, the charge makes her hair stand on end."

"That is so cool," Douggie exclaimed as he approached the table with the machine on it. "Can I try?" he said with a huge smile on his face.

"Of course, you may. Come around and stand on the stool," responded the docent. As Douggie came around the table, the docent helped the young girl down from the stool. "Now, place both hands on the ball and watch what happens," the docent said to Douggie.

As Douggie did what she said, he felt his hair lift upwards and he felt a slight tingling on his scalp. "This feels funny," Douggie stated, still holding onto the ball.

"You ought to see what it is doing to your hair, Douggie," his father exclaimed, laughing at his son from the other side of the table. His mother was also enjoying the crazy results of this machine on her son's hair as she pointed and covered her mouth to hide her giggling.

The docent explained how a charge built up on his body, waiting for a place to go. She called this buildup of charge static electricity, meaning it was not flowing anywhere. Next, she asked if she could touch his arm. Douggie reluctantly agreed, not knowing what was going to happen, but he figured it wouldn't be too bad or she wouldn't do it. When she touched his arm a few things happened. A spark shot out between his arm and the docent's finger, and his hair dropped a little bit but soon went back up.

Douggie reacted, "Ouch! That hurt," but the smile on his face indicated that it really didn't hurt much at all. "It felt like the shocks we give each other when we walk across the carpet and touch someone," Douggie added, still holding on to the metal ball. "Can I get down now?" He asked the docent.

"Sure. Here, watch your step," the docent said as she reached out to hold an arm as he stepped down.

"That was really cool," Douggie said to the docent as he returned to the other side of the demonstration table. "What's the balloon for?" he asked the docent, motioning to the big red balloon sitting on the table. "It demonstrates how static electric forces can build up between the balloon and your hair. It has a similar affect as this Van de Graff generator does," the docent stated, picking up the balloon and handing it to Douggie. "Just rub it on your hair for twenty seconds, then slowly lift it up and it will pull your hair up with it."

Douggie began rubbing his hair with the balloon as other people started gathering around to see what would happen. Once he had built up a charge on the balloon, Douggie slowly started pulling the balloon off his head and the hair looked like it was stuck to the balloon.

"Why does it do that?" Douggie asked the docent, as he placed the balloon back on the table.

"The balloon builds up a charge difference between itself and your hair. The balloon is attracted to the opposite charges in your hair, pulling it towards the balloon." the docent answered. "The balloon can also pick up confetti. Try it," the docent said, as she motioned towards a pile of confetti.

Douggie picked up large amounts of confetti by holding the balloon close to the pile. "This is amazing!" Douggie exclaimed as he cleaned off all the confetti and placed the balloon back on the table. "Thank you for showing me this," Douggie said, as he turned around and started leaving the center.

As they were moving away from the center, Alfred approached Douggie and asked, "Did you have a great time, me Laddie?"

"Yes, and I learned so much," Douggie responded. "It was quite shocking," Douggie said with his best British accent. His attempt at a British accent caused everyone to smile.

"I'm sure it was. Don't forget to watch the video on the Nicola Tesla. It's electrifying," Alfred responded with a giant smile on his face.

As Douggie and his parents made their way through the hall to the next exhibit, Douggie began thinking about building his own electromagnet to see just how strong he could make it. "Dad, can we stop at the hardware store on our way home? I have some materials I would like to use on my next project."

His father looked down at Douggie and smiled. "Sure, if they're not too expensive." His parents looked at each other with strained smiles and whispered, "Here we go again."

Questions:

1. Why did all the paper clips fall when the docent unhooked one of the wires to the electromagnet?
2. What is the relationship between the number of coils and the strength of the electromagnet?
3. What is the relationship between the North Pole and the South Pole ends of a magnet?
4. What caused the shock when the docent touched Douggie's arm?

Vocabulary:

1. Electromagnet
2. Permanent magnet
3. Static electricity
4. Van De Graff generator

Chapter 15

MAGNETIC FIXES

PS2-4: Define a simple design problem that may be
solved by applying scientific ideas about magnets.

Saturdays were usually work days at Douggie's house. Douggie's
mother would generate a list of projects which needed either cleaning
or fixing, to help keep the house in top shape. The list was usually full
of a variety of jobs. Some were regulars, but there were always a few jobs
Douggie never anticipated. He actually enjoyed crossing items off the
list, and making the whole process a bit more fun.

For this Saturday, Douggie's mother had asked if both Douggie and
his father could help fix the linen closet door. It wouldn't stay closed
anymore, and Douggie's mother needed their help. Douggie and his
father looked at the long door, which was approximately four feet tall,
and they both saw the problem right away. The long wooden door was
warped, or it had changed its shape and it no longer closed flat against
the closet frame. Douggie was able to push the door closed, but as soon
as he let go, the door pulled away from the frame.

Douggie sat on the floor and took out the neodymium magnets his
mother had bought him at the science center. He started pulling them
apart and putting them back together, trying to fill the time with an
activity while his father came up with the perfect idea to fix their little
problem. He knew his father would soon find an answer and they would
be fixing it shortly, making his mother happy. As the waiting continued,
Douggie began putting one magnet on the floor and bringing the other

magnets close enough to make it jump off the floor and back into the stack of his little magnets.

His father knew an easy fix was only a thought away. Unfortunately, that thought hadn't entered his mind yet. He simply stared at the door for a few minutes and hoped something would come to him. The noise the magnets were making caught his attention and he looked down at what his son was doing. As he watched Douggie play with the magnets, an idea popped into his mind.

"I think I've figured it out. May I use a few of those magnets?" Douggie's father asked.

"Sure, I have a whole stack of them," Douggie replied, glad he could actually be of some help.

"I'm going to need to drill a few holes to inset the magnets, making them even with the wood frame and the door. These magnets are strong and should easily hold the door if I used two at the top and two at the bottom," his father stated, rubbing his chin and thinking out loud.

"I'll go get the drill and drill bits," Douggie said as he ran to the garage.

"Don't forget the glue," his father yelled, hoping to save a trip to the garage.

As his father measured and marked the placement of the holes he needed to drill, Douggie got the magnets and the glue ready for when his father needed them. Douggie figured out the magnets had to be pointed in the correct direction or they would repel one another rather than attract.

"Each magnet was approximately one centimeter in diameter and a quarter of a centimeter thick," his father stated, thinking out loud again. Looking through his various drill bits he found one that matched perfectly.

Once the holes were drilled, the next step was to put some strong glue in the hole to hold the magnet tightly.

"Dad, these are really strong magnets. Won't they just pull out when we try to open the doors?" Douggie asked with a look of concern on his face.

"If we use this special glue, it should be strong enough to hold the magnets and keep them from coming out of the holes when the doors are opened again," said his father. "We just need to make sure the glue dries completely before we try to use the door."

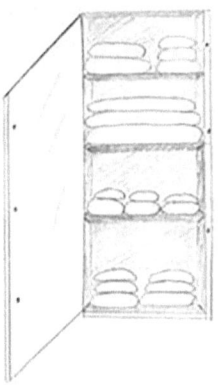

"Can I put the glue in the holes, Dad?" Douggie asked.

"Ok, but you need to be careful not to spill it. It comes out fast and I don't want you to get any on you," his father stated.

Once the glue was in and the small magnets placed into the holes, Douggie and his father left them to dry. "What else can we fix with these magnets?" Douggie asked.

"Well, the arm rest in my car has a broken latch needing fixing," his father suggested.

"Do you think these magnets can be used to fix your latch?" Douggie asked, with an excited look on his face. Douggie liked fixing things with his father.

"We could try. Are you sure you don't mind using more of those little magnets of yours?" His father asked.

"If this works, we will have fixed two problems in one day. I think that is a good use for these little guys," he said looking down at the remaining six magnets in his hand.

His father smiled and said, "Let's do it, then. No time like the present."

This particular fix would not need any drilling. Since the connection was not flush with the lid, but down a few centimeters, they were going to have to glue five of the little magnets together and attach them to the inside of the chamber, and then glue the last one to the lid of the arm rest directly above the other five. This time Douggie's father handled the glue because he didn't want Douggie to glue his fingers together.

Douggie held the lid of the armrest at an angle so his father could easily glue on the magnet. Once they glued the magnet on the lid, Douggie released the lid and it opened up due to the strong spring attached to the hinge.

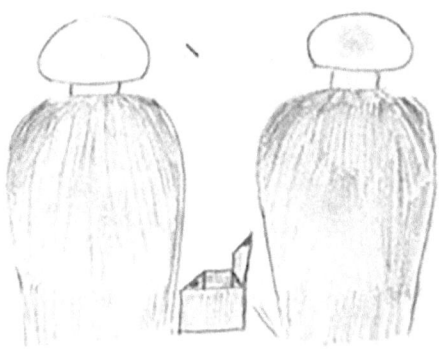

The next part of the fix was the most difficult. It required his father to glue five magnets together and then glue them to a small flat area inside the chamber directly under the magnet on the lid. If they were not placed exactly in the perfect position, the magnets wouldn't hold on to each other and the spring would cause the lid to fly open again. Douggie's father decided to let the glue on the single magnet, attached to the lid, completely dry first. He then was able to magnetically attach the other five glued magnets to the single magnet on the lid. With a small amount of glue added to the bottom of the set of five magnets, he was able to shut the lid and guarantee all the magnets lined up. The final challenge was to keep the lid closed while the glue on the bottom of the magnets dried.

Douggie had an idea. He ran and got one of his father's weights from his barbell set. "Ten pounds should do the trick," Douggie said as he looked through the different sized weights. His father had just finished gluing as Douggie arrived with the weight.

"Put the weight on top of the lid, Son."

"Perfect," Douggie exclaimed. "Dad this is fun. Now let's go see if the linen doors close and open correctly."

They both rushed inside to see if their idea had worked. His father closed the door and the magnets latched perfectly.

"Now, the real test is if we can open the door without pulling the magnets out of their holes," his father stated, looking concerned.

They both opened the door together and the magnets stayed glued in, just as they had hoped.

"Dad, it worked!" Douggie said, almost yelling with excitement. "It sure did, Douggie. Now we have one more thing to do," his dad said looking down at his son. "We need to find a way to unglue my fingers," his dad said with a smile on his face. Douggie and his father laughed as they made their way to the garage to find a solution to their new problem.

Questions:

1. Other than the simple round magnets used to fix these problems, what else could be used to accomplish the same results?
2. Why was Douggie concerned the glue would not hold the magnets in place in the linen closet?
3. What could have caused the wooden door to warp?
4. Is there another way they could have attached the magnets in the car's arm rest?

Vocabulary:

1. Flush
2. Latched
3. Repel

www.ingramcontent.com/pod-product-compliance
Lightning Source LLC
Chambersburg PA
CBHW020424130626
46549CB00006B/2732